DATE DUE

Emily Dickinson

These and other titles are included in The Importance Of
biography series:

Alexander the Great	Adolf Hitler
Muhammad Ali	Harry Houdini
Louis Armstrong	Thomas Jefferson
James Baldwin	Mother Jones
Clara Barton	Chief Joseph
The Beatles	Joe Louis
Napoleon Bonaparte	Malcolm X
Julius Caesar	Thurgood Marshall
Rachel Carson	Margaret Mead
Charlie Chaplin	Golda Meir
Charlemagne	Michelangelo
Cesar Chavez	Wolfgang Amadeus Mozart
Winston Churchill	John Muir
Cleopatra	Sir Isaac Newton
Christopher Columbus	Richard M. Nixon
Hernando Cortes	Georgia O'Keeffe
Marie Curie	Louis Pasteur
Charles Dickens	Pablo Picasso
Emily Dickinson	Elvis Presley
Amelia Earhart	Jackie Robinson
Thomas Edison	Norman Rockwell
Albert Einstein	Eleanor Roosevelt
Duke Ellington	Anwar Sadat
Dian Fossey	Margaret Sanger
Benjamin Franklin	Oskar Schindler
Galileo Galilei	John Steinbeck
Emma Goldman	Tecumseh
Jane Goodall	Jim Thorpe
Martha Graham	Mark Twain
Lorraine Hansberry	Queen Victoria
Stephen Hawking	Pancho Villa
Jim Henson	H. G. Wells

Emily Dickinson

by
Bradley Steffens

Lucent Books, P.O. Box 289011, San Diego, CA 92198-9011

Library of Congress Cataloging-in-Publication Data

Steffens, Bradley, 1956–
     Emily Dickinson / by Bradley Steffens.
        p.   cm. — (The importance of)
     Includes bibliographical references (p.   ) and index.
     Summary: Describes the life, work, and significance of the
poet of Amherst.
        ISBN 1-56006-089-1 (alk. paper)
        1. Dickinson, Emily, 1830–1886—Juvenile literature. 2.
     Women poets, American—19th century—Biography—Juvenile
     literature. [1. Dickinson, Emily, 1830–1886. 2. Poets, American.
     3. Women—Biography.]   I. Title.   II. Series.
PS1541.Z5S84   1998
811'.4—dc21   97–21373
[B]   CIP
                                                             AC

Copyright 1998 by Lucent Books, Inc., P.O. Box 289011,
San Diego, California 92198-9011

Printed in the U.S.A.

In memory of Roger K. Blakely,
poet, preceptor, and friend

Contents

Foreword   9

Important Dates in the Life of Emily Dickinson   10

INTRODUCTION
A Miracle of Creativity   11

CHAPTER 1
Home   13

CHAPTER 2
Heavenly Hurt   24

CHAPTER 3
A Friend Who Taught Immortality   32

CHAPTER 4
Poet   41

CHAPTER 5
Preceptor   52

CHAPTER 6
The Soul Selects Her Own Society   60

CHAPTER 7
Distant Strains of Triumph   68

EPILOGUE
If Fame Belonged to Me   76

Notes   84

For Further Reading   89

Works Consulted   90

Index   92

Credits   95

About the Author   96

Foreword

THE IMPORTANCE OF biography series deals with individuals who have made a unique contribution to history. The editors of the series have deliberately chosen to cast a wide net and include people from all fields of endeavor. Individuals from politics, music, art, literature, philosophy, science, sports, and religion are all represented. In addition, the editors did not restrict the series to individuals whose accomplishments have helped change the course of history. Of necessity, this criterion would have eliminated many whose contribution was great, though limited. Charles Darwin, for example, was responsible for radically altering the scientific view of the natural history of the world. His achievements continue to impact the study of science today. Others, such as Chief Joseph of the Nez Percé, played a pivotal role in the history of their own people. While Joseph's influence does not extend much beyond the Nez Percé, his nonviolent resistance to white expansion and his continuing role in protecting his tribe and his homeland remain an inspiration to all.

These biographies are more than factual chronicles. Each volume attempts to emphasize an individual's contributions both in his or her own time and for posterity. For example, the voyages of Christopher Columbus opened the way to European colonization of the New World. Unquestionably, his encounter with the New World brought monumental changes to both Europe and the Americas in his day. Today, however, the broader impact of Columbus's voyages is being critically scrutinized. *Christopher Columbus,* as well as every biography in The Importance Of series, includes and evaluates the most recent scholarship available on each subject.

Each author includes a wide variety of primary and secondary source quotations to document and substantiate his or her work. All quotes are footnoted to show readers exactly how and where biographers derive their information, as well as provide stepping stones to further research. These quotations enliven the text by giving readers eyewitness views of the life and times of each individual covered in The Importance Of series.

Finally, each volume is enhanced by photographs, bibliographies, chronologies, and comprehensive indexes. For both the casual reader and the student engaged in research, The Importance Of biographies will be a fascinating adventure into the lives of people who have helped shape humanity's past and present, and who will continue to shape its future.

IMPORTANT DATES IN THE LIFE OF EMILY DICKINSON

1830
Emily Elizabeth Dickinson born.

1840
Edward Dickinson, Emily's father, sells his half of the Homestead; family moves to North Pleasant Street; Emily and her sister Lavinia enroll in Amherst Academy.

1847
Emily enrolls at Mount Holyoke Female Seminary.

1848
Emily leaves Mount Holyoke after one year, meets Ben Newton.

1850
The *Indicator* publishes Emily's prose valentine; Emily composes her earliest surviving poem, "Awake ye muses nine."

1852
The Springfield *Daily Republican* publishes "'Sic transit gloria mundi'"; Edward Dickinson is elected to U.S. House of Representatives.

1853
Ben Newton dies.

1855
Edward Dickinson repurchases the Homestead.

1856
Emily's brother, Austin, marries Susan Gilbert.

1860
Charles Wadsworth calls on Emily.

1861
The Springfield *Daily Republican* publishes "I taste a liquor never brewed," retitled "The May-Wine."

1862
The Springfield *Daily Republican* publishes "Safe in their Alabaster Chambers," retitled "The Sleeping"; Emily writes first letters to Thomas Wentworth Higginson.

1864
The Springfield *Daily Republican* publishes "Blazing in gold, and quenching in purple," retitled "Sunset"; the *Round Table* publishes "Some keep the Sabbath going to church," retitled "My Sabbath."

1866
The Springfield *Daily Republican* publishes "A narrow Fellow in the Grass," retitled "The Snake."

1874
Edward Dickinson dies.

1875
Emily Norcross Dickinson, Emily's mother, is paralyzed.

1876
Helen Hunt Jackson asks Emily for a poem to be published anonymously.

1878
"Success is counted sweetest," retitled "Success," appears in *A Masque of Poets.*

1882
Charles Wadsworth dies; Emily Norcross Dickinson dies; Mabel Loomis Todd befriends Emily and Lavinia.

1886
Emily dies on May 15.

1890
Roberts Brothers publishes *Poems* by Emily Dickinson.

1891
Roberts Brothers publishes *Poems, Second Series* by Emily Dickinson.

1894
First edition of *Letters of Emily Dickinson* published.

1896
Third series of *Poems* published by Roberts Brothers.

1955
The Complete Poems of Emily Dickinson published.

A Miracle of Creativity

On December 10, 1830, Emily Norcross Dickinson, the daughter of Joel and Betsy Norcross, gave birth to her second child in the family's large brick home on Main Street in Amherst, Massachusetts. Mrs. Dickinson and her husband, Edward, already had a one-year-old boy named William Austin. Their second child was a girl. They named her Emily Elizabeth.

Two years and two months later, Mrs. Dickinson gave birth to her third and last child, a girl named Lavinia. Seven years af-terward, the Dickinson family moved out of the family homestead on Main Street and into a wood-framed house on North Pleasant Street.

Emily Elizabeth Dickinson did not en-joy the best of health as a child, but she, her brother, and her sister all lived well into adulthood. In 1855 their father re-purchased the brick house on Main Street, and the family returned to the Dickinson Homestead. William Austin, who was called Austin, eventually married and moved

The house on North Pleasant Street where the Dickinsons lived from 1840 to 1855.

A portrait of Emily, Austin, and Lavinia Dickinson painted by O. A. Bullard in 1840. In her left hand, Emily holds a book and a flower—two things she loved throughout her life.

away. Emily and Lavinia, who was known as Vinnie, never did. They lived together in their parents' home until they died.

From all outward appearances, nothing unusual happened in the large house on Main Street in the thirty-one years after the Dickinson family returned to it. Appearances can be deceiving, however, as Emily herself often observed. Between 1855 and 1886, a miracle of human creativity occurred within the sturdy brick walls of the Dickinson Homestead. Emily Elizabeth Dickinson composed no fewer than 1,775 poems, including a few that many readers and literary critics consider to be among the very best ever written by an American poet.

The creation of so many fine poems is itself an achievement worthy of biography, but Dickinson did more than make beautiful works of art. She wrote a kind of poetry that was different from the work of other poets of her time. Her poems are more succinct and less sentimental than those of many of her contemporaries. In addition, Dickinson tried and perfected techniques that few poets had used before her, but many have adopted since. Ignoring the norms of prosody and sometimes even the rules of grammar itself, she bent the English language to conform to her unique vision of the world. By doing so, she helped free herself—and succeeding generations of poets—from the tyranny of poetic convention. Her tough-minded and idiosyncratic approach to the art of writing made Emily Dickinson the first truly modern American poet.

1 Home

"Home was always dear to me," Emily Dickinson wrote to her brother, Austin, when she was a teenager away at school, and so it must have been. No home is perfect, of course, but the picture Emily painted of hers makes it seem idyllic:

> When tempted to feel sad, I think of the blazing fire, & the cheerful meal & the chair empty now I am gone. I can hear the cheerful voices and the merry laugh & a desolate feeling comes home to my heart, to think I am alone.[1]

By all accounts, Emily Dickinson's childhood was a happy one. When she was two years old, her parents sent her to stay with her aunt Lavinia for a few weeks. In a letter to Emily's mother, Aunt Lavinia wrote that her niece was "very affectionate & we all love her very much." A few days later, in another letter, Aunt Lavinia added, "She is well I believe & appears perfectly contented—There never was a better child."[2]

The letters Emily wrote as a child reveal her to be a high-spirited girl with a wonderful sense of humor. In May 1842, when she was twelve, Emily wrote to her friend Jane Humphrey about a classmate's speech. Emily's account of the boy's speech (and her response to it) reveals her sharp wit:

> This Afternoon is Wednesday and so of course there was Speaking and Com-position—there was one young man who read a Composition. [T]he Subject was think twice before you speak—he was describing the reasons why any one should do so—one was—if a young gentleman—offered a young lady his arm and he had a dog who had no tail and he boarded at the tavern think twice before you speak. Another is if a young gentleman knows a young lady who he thinks nature has formed to perfection let him remember that roses conceal thorns[.] [H]e is the sillyest [sic] creature that ever lived I think. I told him that I thought he had better think twice before he spoke[.][3]

At the time she wrote this letter, Emily was enrolled at Amherst Academy, a private grammar school. The academy had been founded twenty-eight years earlier by Emily's grandfather Samuel Fowler Dickinson. At a time when many schools allowed only boys to enroll, Amherst Academy welcomed both male and female students. Samuel Fowler Dickinson believed that parents should educate their daughters as well as their sons. He expressed these views in a speech he gave to the Hampshire, Hampden, and Franklin Agricultural Society a few months after Emily was born.

A good husbandman will also *educate well his daughters.* I distinguish the education of daughters from that of sons; because, Nature has designed them to occupy places, in family, and in society, altogether dissimilar.

"You Must Write Oftener to Us"

First published in The Letters of Emily Dickinson, *edited by Thomas H. Johnson and Theodora Ward, this is the earliest surviving letter written by the poet. Emily gave this letter to her father to take to her brother, Austin, who was enrolled in Williston Seminary in Northampton, Massachusetts. Emily was eleven years old at the time.*

"Amherst Mass. April 18 1842

My dear Brother

As Father was going to Northampton and thought of coming over to see you I thought I would improve the opportunity and write you a few lines— We miss you very much indeed you cannot think how odd it seems without you. . . . the Hens get along nicely the chickens grow very fast I am afraid they will be so large that you cannot perceive them with the naked Eye when you get home the yellow hen is coming off with a brood of chickens we found a hens nest with four Eggs in it I took out three and brought them in the next day I went to see if there had been any laid and there had not been any laid and the one that was there had gone so I suppose a skonk [*sic*] had been there or else a hen In the shape of a skonk and I dont know which— the Hens lay finely William gets two a day at his house we 5 or 6 a day here there Is one Creeper that lays on the ground the nests are so high that they cannot reach them from the ground I Expect we shall have to make some ladders for them to get up on. . . . we received your letter Friday morning and very glad we were to get it you must write oftener to us. . . . we are all very well and hope you are the same—we have very pleasant weather now Mr Whipple has come and we expect Miss Humphrey tomorrow— Aunt Montague—has been saying you would cry before the week was out Cousin Zebina had a fit the other day and bit his tongue into— as you say it is a rainy day and I can think of— Nothing more to say— I shall Expect an answer to my letter soon. . . . all send a great deal of love to you and hope you are getting along well and— Enjoy your self

Your affectionate Sister Emily—"

Amherst Academy, the private school founded by Emily Dickinson's grandfather, Samuel Fowler Dickinson. Emily, Austin, and Lavinia all attended the three-story school.

Daughters should be *well instructed*, in the useful sciences; comprising a *good* English education: including a thorough knowledge of our own language, geography, history, mathematics, and natural philosophy. The female mind, so sensitive, so susceptible of improvement, should not be neglected. . . . God hath designed nothing in vain.[4]

Emily Dickinson thrived in the academic environment her grandfather helped create.

The curriculum of Amherst Academy was more rigorous than that of the town's one-room public school, and Emily was proud of it. "We have a very fine school," Emily wrote to her close friend Abiah Root in 1845. "I have four studies. There are Mental Philosophy, Geology, Latin, and Botany. How large they sound, don't they? I don't believe you have such big studies."[5]

According to Frederick Tuckerman, a historian of the school, Amherst Academy offered several language arts classes, including reading, grammar, declamation, rhetoric, and composition. It also offered a range of social studies classes: ancient and modern geography, sacred geography, general history, and history of the United States. Science and philosophy were covered in depth. Students were expected to complete courses in natural philosophy, chemistry, moral philosophy, and intellectual philosophy. Mathematics rounded out the curriculum. Dickinson and her classmates studied intellectual and written arithmetic and algebra. They also learned practical mathematical skills, such as comprehending navigation, surveying, measurement, and astronomical calculations.[6] Dickinson studied foreign languages as well, including Latin and German. Later Dickinson would use concepts and images from many if not all of these subjects in her poetry. Her years at Amherst Academy gave her poetry a richness and variety that one might not otherwise expect from a young woman who grew up in rural Massachusetts before the Civil War.

Sacred Subjects

Although the subjects offered at Amherst Acadd emy appear to be secular, or nonre-

Emily Dickinson as she appeared at the age of nine. Her fine lace collar shows that she came from a well-to-do family.

Mathematics . . . forms the very framework of nature's harmonies, and is essential to the argument for a God. . . . [Chemistry] abounds with the most beautiful exhibitions of the Divine wisdom and benevolence. . . . The wide dominions of natural history, embracing zoology, botany, and mineralogy, the theologist has even found crowded with demonstrations of the Divine Existence and of God's Providential care and government.[7]

Emily absorbed the religious thought of her day, and it colored almost everything she wrote. In another letter to Abiah Root, the fifteen-year-old Dickinson worried that she and her friend had broken God's law because they had not made wise use of their time:

How swiftly summer has fled & what report has it borne to heaven of misspent time & wasted hours? Eternity only will answer. The ceaseless flight of the seasons is to me a very solemn thought, & yet Why do we not strive to make a better improvement of them? . . . For God has said. "Work while the day lasts for the night is coming in which no man can work."

Dickinson then suggested that she and Abiah make an effort to mend their ways. "Let us strive together to part with time more reluctantly,"[8] she wrote.

Emily learned most of what she knew about God, time, and eternity not at school, nor at church, but at home. Every morning Emily's father, Edward Dickinson, led the family in prayers and read from the Bible. An attorney who served in the Massachusetts state legislature and the U.S. House of Representatives, Edward

ligious, they were not. Samuel Fowler Dickinson founded the academy as a Christian school, and religion permeated all the subjects taught there. Some courses, such as "sacred geography," were strictly devoted to religious topics. Even courses that might appear to have little to do with religion, such as mathematics chemistry, were informed with Christian thought.

The Christians who founded and taught at the school believed that since God created the universe, any study of the world would reveal His divine presence within it. Edward Hitchcock, president of Amherst College—another school founded by Samuel Fowler Dickinson—expressed these widely held beliefs in his inauguration speech of 1845:

A Visit to Boston

While visiting her aunt in Boston, Emily sent this letter, included in The Letters of Emily Dickinson, *to her close friend Abiah Root.*

"Boston. Sep. 8. 1846.

My dear friend Abiah.

It is a long—long time since I received your welcome letter & it becomes me to sue for forgiveness, which I am sure your affectionate heart will not refuse to grant. . . . I have been here a fortnight today & in that time I have both seen & heard a great many wonderful things. Perhaps you might like to know how I have spent the time here. I have been to Mount Auburn, to the Chinese Museum, to Bunker hill. I have attended 2 concerts, & 1 Horticultural exhibition. . . .

The Chinese Museum is a great curiosity. There are an endless variety of Wax figures made to resemble the Chinese & dressed in their costume. . . . Two of the Chinese go with this exhibition. One of them is a Professor of music in China & the other is a teacher of a writing school at home. They were both wealthy & not obliged to labor but they were also Opium Eaters & fearing to continue the practice lest it destroyed their lives yet unable to break the 'rigid chain of habit' in their own land They left their family's & came to this country. They have now entirely overcome the practice. There is something peculiarly interesting to me in their self *denial*. . . . The Writing Master is constantly occupied in writing the names of visitors who request it upon cards in the Chinese language—for which he charges 12-½ cts. apiece. He never fails to give his card besides to the person who wish it. I obtained one of his cards for Viny [Lavinia] & myself & I consider them very precious. . . .

Do write me soon Dear A & let it be a long—long letter. Dont forget—!!!!!

Your aff. friend
Emily E.D."

Dickinson possessed the practiced voice of a public speaker. He read the Bible with vigor and passion. Years later, after her father's death, Emily recalled the intensity of these daily readings: "'I say unto you,' Father would read Prayers, with a militant Accent that would startle one."[9]

These daily readings not only shaped Emily's religious faith, but they also nurtured her growing love of language. Her father read a version of the Bible known as the King James Bible. Written in 1607, the King James Bible possesses a rich vocabulary and beautiful rhythms that make it the most poetic version of the Bible ever written in English. Emily owned her own copy of the King James Bible. She marked many passages in the small leather-bound volume. She referred to, quoted, and paraphrased the Bible in her letters and poetry far more than any other book. In a letter to Abiah Root, for example, she quotes Christ's words to his disciples, writing, "'Yet a little while I am with you, and again a little while and I am *not* with you' because you go to your mother!"[10] Such citations are sometimes serious, sometimes humorous, and sometimes in between, depending on the mood Dickinson was in or the effect she intended her words to have.

Emily's father, Edward Dickinson, was known as one of the leading citizens of Amherst. O. A. Bullard painted this portrait of him in 1840.

A Prominent Family

Emily's father led the family not only in their prayers, but in every other way as well. In 1870 the *Amherst Record*, the local newspaper, called him the town's leading citizen.

> HONORABLE EDWARD DICKINSON. If there is a native of Amherst to whom the name at the head of this article is a stranger, he must indeed be a curiosity. . . . The name of Dickinson . . . is so identified with everything that belongs to Amherst, that any attempt to speak of the town history in which that name should not appear the most prominent would be impossible. . . . We believe we transgress no law of propriety in claiming him to be the most prominent of the living men in Amherst.[11]

A history of the college praised him for being "one of the firmest pillars of society,

A Last Visit to a Friend

When Emily Dickinson was fourteen, her close friend Sophia Holland, also fourteen, died. Two years later, Dickinson described her friend's death in a letter to Abiah Root, published in The Letters of Emily Dickinson.

"I have never lost but one friend near my age & with whom my thoughts & her own were the same. It was before you came to Amherst. My friend was Sophia Holland. She was too lovely for earth & she was transplanted from earth to heaven. I visited her often in sickness & watched over her bed. But at length Reason fled and the physician forbid any but the nurse to go into her room. Then it seemed to me I should die too if I could not be permitted to watch over her or even to look at her face. At length the doctor said she must die & allowed me to look at her a moment through the open door. I took off my shoes and stole softly to the sick room.

There she lay mild & beautiful as in health & her pale features lit up with an unearthly—smile. I looked as long as friends would permit & when they told me I must look no longer I let them lead me away. I shed no tear, for my heart was too full to weep, but after she was laid in her coffin & I felt I could not call her back again I gave way to a fixed melancholy.

I told no one the cause of my grief, though it was gnawing at my very heart strings. I was not well & I went to Boston & stayed a month & my health improved so that my spirits were better. I trust she is now in heaven & though I shall never forget her, yet I shall meet her in heaven."

education, order, morality, and every good cause in our community."[12] In addition to being a respected lawyer and elected official, Edward Dickinson served as the treasurer of Amherst College for thirty-eight years. His financial leadership may have saved the college. According to Stanley King, a historian, the college was "deeply in debt" when Edward Dickinson took control of its finances. "Its friends were in grave doubt as to whether the College could in fact survive," King writes. "At the end of his term, the College had assets over a million dollars."[13]

Edward Dickinson also helped bring the first railroad to Amherst, served as a volunteer in the fire brigade, and led the community in a number of social causes, including the temperance movement.

Just as he had followed in his own father's footsteps, Edward Dickinson expected his children—especially his son,

Austin—to follow in his. He set high standards for their education, sending all three of his children to private grammar school and then to college.

The Dickinsons at Home

Stern, formal, and somewhat aloof, Edward Dickinson nevertheless cherished his family. Emily knew that beneath her father's woolen suit beat a warm and sometimes sentimental heart. In a letter she wrote to Austin when he was away at Harvard Law School, Emily captured the tenderness beneath her father's sober exterior:

> Father takes great delight in your remarks to him—puts on his spectacles and reads them o'er and o'er as if it were a blessing to have an only son.

> He reads all the letters you write, as soon as he gets [them], at the post-office, no matter to whom addressed. . . . Well, I was telling you, he reads them once at the office, then he makes me read them loud at the supper table again, and when he gets home in the evening, he cracks a few walnuts, puts his spectacles on, and with your last in his hand, sits down to enjoy the evening. . . .

> I do think it's so funny—you and father do nothing but "fisticuff" [fight] all the while you're at home, and the minute you are separated, you become such devoted friends; but this is a checkered life.

> I believe at this moment, Austin, that there's no body living for whom father has such respect as for you, and yet your conduct together is quite peculiar indeed.[14]

This letter seems to refute the notion, advanced by Millicent Todd Bingham and others, that Edward Dickinson ruled the household like a tyrant. In her book *Emily Dickinson's Home*, Bingham, whose mother was a close friend of the family, writes of Edward Dickinson, "No one openly opposed his decisions, least of all the family. He knew what was right and what was wrong and that was the end of it. As his daughter Emily remarked, 'What Father says he means.'"[15] Emily's letter to her brother, however, makes it clear that Austin was more than willing to stand up to his father. Another story told by Bingham suggests that Emily had her own ways of commenting on, if not directly opposing, her father's will.

> One day, sitting down at the dinner table, he inquired whether a certain nicked plate must always be placed before him. Emily took the hint. She carried the plate to the garden and pulverized it on a stone, "just to remind" her, she said, not to give it to her father again.[16]

Richard B. Sewall, a biographer of Dickinson, believes the episode of the chipped plate shows Emily "as a master strategist, replying to [her father's] imperiousness with a humor and dispatch he could not have missed."[17]

Emily saw a deep contrast between her father's stern public image and the softer side he revealed at home, and she enjoyed pointing it out. In another letter to Austin, Emily described the scene as her father went out in his nightclothes to get wood for the fire:

> The meat and potato and a little pan of your favorite brown bread are keeping warm at the fire while father goes

for shavings. . . . He wore a palm leaf hat and his pantaloons tucked in his boots and I couldn't help thinking of you as he strode along by the window. I don't think negligée quite becoming to so mighty a man.[18]

Like her husband, Emily Norcross Dickinson doted on her children. While Austin was attending Harvard Law School, Emily provided him with another example of how much their parents missed him. As usual, Emily could not resist poking a little fun at her parents:

Mother is warming her feet, which she assures me confidently are "just as cold as ice.["] I tell her I fear there is a danger of icification, or ossification—I dont [sic] know certainly which. Father is reading the Bible—I take it for consolation, judging from outward things. He and mother take great delight in dwelling upon your character, and reviewing your many virtues, and Father's prayers for you at our morning devotions are enough to break one's heart—it is really very touching; surely "our blessings brighten" the farther off they fly! Mother wipes her eyes with the end of her linen apron, and consoles herself by thinking of several future places "where congregations ne'er break up" and Austins have no end![19]

One of the greatest gifts the Dickinsons gave to their children, perhaps without their ever realizing it, was access to their library. The Dickinson family library contained nearly one thousand books, one of the largest collections in Amherst. Emily spent countless hours exploring it.

In a time before radio, television, motion pictures, and the Internet, the main source of information about the outside world came from printed matter—books, magazines, and newspapers. The Dickinsons were charter subscribers to *The Atlantic Monthly*, published then as now in Boston. They also subscribed to a number of other periodicals, including the Springfield *Daily Republican*, the newspaper of the nearest large town. The arrival of a new book at the local bookstore was important enough news for Emily to include in a letter to her friend and future sister-in-law Susan Gilbert. "Longfellow's 'golden Legend' has come to town I hear," Emily wrote, "and may be seen *in state* on Mr. Adams' bookshelves."[20]

From her girlhood on, books were Dickinson's constant companions. She once referred to her copy of Ralph Waldo Emerson's poems as "a granite little book

Emily's mother, Emily Norcross Dickinson, doted on her children but, as Emily later observed, did "not care for thought."

you can lean on."[21] In addition to the works of Longfellow and Emerson, she read the poetry of William Shakespeare, John Keats, Robert Browning, and Elizabeth Barrett Browning; the novels of the Brontë sisters; the essays of John Ruskin; and many other works by major and minor authors. In one of her poems, she refers to books as her "Kinsmen of the Shelf."[22] In another, she portrays a book as a living being who takes her back in time:

> A precious—mouldering pleasure—'tis—
> To meet an Antique Book—
> In just the Dress his Century wore—
> A privilege—I think—
>
> His venerable Hand to take—
> And warming in our own—
> A passage back—or two—to make
> To Times when he—was young—
>
> His quaint opinions—to inspect—
> His thought to ascertain
> On Themes concern our mutual
>   mind—
> The Literature of Man—
>
> What interested Scholars—most—
> What Competitions ran—
> When Plato—was a Certainty—
> And Sophocles—a Man—
>
> When Sappho—was a living Girl—
> And Beatrice wore
> The Gown that Dante—deified—
> Facts Centuries before
>
> He traverses—familiar—
> As One should come to Town—
> And tell you all your Dreams—
>   were true—
> He lived—where Dreams were born—
>
> His presence is Enchantment—
> You beg him not to go—
> Old Volumes shake their Vellum Heads
> And tantalize—just so—[23]

In one of her most famous poems, Dickinson compares a book to a ship. "There is no Frigate like a Book," she writes, "To take us lands away."[24] The volumes in her family's library carried Emily's active imagination across time and space.

Edward Dickinson shared his daughter's passion for reading, but not her tastes. "My father . . . reads *lonely & rigorous* books," she once wrote to a friend. To Austin, she confided, "We do not have much poetry, father having made up his mind that it[']s pretty much all *real life.*" According to Emily, her father dismissed the work of Emerson, Longfellow, Charles Dickens, Harriet Beecher Stowe, and other popular writers as "*nothing*, compared to past generations, who flourished *when he was a boy.*" To get around their father's narrow taste, Emily, Austin, and Lavinia once hid a copy of Longfellow's book *Kavanaugh* inside the family's piano.[25]

A Surprising Kinship

Although Edward Dickinson was generally a calm, practical man, he was once so moved by a spectacle of nature that he could not contain his desire to share it with others. In a letter to Austin, Emily described how their father had used the church bells to summon the entire town to a display of northern lights:

> There was quite an excitement in the village Monday evening. We were all startled by a violent church bell ringing, and thinking of nothing but fire, rushed out in the street to see. The sky was a beautiful red, bordering on crimson, and rays of a gold pink color were

constantly shooting off from a kind of sun in the centre. People were alarmed at the beautiful Phenomenon, supposing that fires somewhere were *coloring the sky*. The exhibition lasted for nearly 15. minutes, and the streets were full of people wondering and admiring. Father happened to see it among the very first and rang the bell *himself* to call attention to it.[26]

The story suggests a surprising kinship between the sober country lawyer and his lively daughter. Throughout her life, Emily Dickinson was deeply moved by the miracles of nature. Like her father beholding the aurora borealis, she often felt an overwhelming desire to share her feelings of awe with others. She never pealed the town's bells to draw attention to a sunset, the flight of a hummingbird, or the passing of a thunderstorm. She did, however, find apt and ringing words that brought these and other wonders to the attention of readers around the world.

2 Heavenly Hurt

In the spring of 1847, when she was sixteen, Emily Dickinson graduated from Amherst Academy. That fall she enrolled at Mount Holyoke Female Seminary, a private religious college for young women. The school is located in South Hadley, ten miles from Amherst. "I am really at Mt Holyoke Seminary & this is to be my home for a long year," Emily wrote to Abiah Root in November 1847. Not surprisingly, Emily missed her family. "I was very homesick for a few days & it seemed to me I could not live here. But I am now contented & quite happy if I can be happy when absent from my dear home & friends."[27]

Founded by Mary Lyon in 1836, Mount Holyoke was an even more religious school than Amherst Academy. Each morning at nine the students gathered for prayers, and each afternoon Mary Lyon lectured on a religious topic. As at Amherst Academy, the teachers at Mount Holyoke taught every subject with a Christian perspective. Describing Mary Lyon, one teacher at the seminary wrote:

> Her regard for the Bible was so fervent, and her reverence for it so profound, that she would dwell on its beauty and sublimity with deep interest. She would also talk with great

Mount Holyoke Female Seminary as it appeared when Emily Dickinson attended it.

A Day in the Life at Mount Holyoke

In November 1847, Emily Dickinson wrote to Abiah Root from Mount Holyoke Female Seminary. In the letter, number 18 of The Letters of Emily Dickinson, *Dickinson provided her friend with her daily schedule.*

"I will tell you my order of time for the day, as you were so kind as to give me your's. At 6. oclock, we all rise. We breakfast at 7. Our study hours begin at 8. At 9. we all meet in the Seminary Hall, for devotions. At 10-¼. I recite a review of Ancient History, in connection with which we read Goldsmith & Grimshaw. At .11. I recite a lesson in 'Pope's Essay on Man' which is merely transposition. At .12. I practice Calisthenics & and at 12-¼ read until dinner, which is at 12-½ & after dinner, from 1-½ until 2 I sing in Seminary Hall. From 2-¾ until 3-¾. I practise upon the Piano. At 3-¾ I go to Sections, where we give in all accounts for the day, including, Absence—Tardiness—Communications—Breaking Silent Study hours—Receiving Company in our rooms & ten thousand other things, which I will not take time or place to mention. At 4-½. we go into Seminary Hall, & receive advice from Miss. Lyon in the form of a lecture. We have Supper at 6. & silent-study hours from then until the retiring bell, which rings at 8-¾, but the tardy bell does not ring until 9-¾, so that we don't often obey the first warning to retire."

delight of the principles of natural religion; and when instructing in natural philosophy, astronomy, &c., she never omitted an opportunity of impressing on the minds of her pupils the power, wisdom, and goodness of God, as displayed in his works.[28]

The other faculty members at Mount Holyoke strove to teach with the same religious zeal displayed by Mary Lyon.

At first, Emily was delighted with the school. "I love this Seminary," she wrote to Abiah Root, "& all the teachers are bound to my heart by ties of affection." She enjoyed the subjects as well. "I am now studying 'Sillman's Chemistry' & Cutler's Physiology, in both of which I am interested," she added. She did not take her studies too seriously, however. To her brother, she joked, "Your *welcome* letter found me all engrossed in the history of Sulphuric Acid!!!!!"[29]

Dickinson's intelligence was readily apparent upon her arrival at the seminary. All new students took entrance examinations at the beginning of the term. Emily passed hers easily, even though she wrote

Mary Lyon, the founder of Mount Holyoke Female Seminary. Lyon possessed a religious zeal that impressed her colleagues and inspired many of her students.

to Abiah Root that the tests were said to be more rigorous than those of previous years.

> I finished them in three days & found them about what I had anticipated, though the old scholars say they are more strict than they ever have been before. . . . Perhaps you know that Miss. Lyon is raising her standard of scholarship a good deal, on account of the number of applicants this year & on account of that she makes the examinations more severe than usual.
>
> You cannot imagine how trying they are, because if we cannot go through them all in a specified time, we are sent home. I cannot be too thankful

that I got through as soon as I did, & I am sure that I never would endure the suspense of which I endured during those three days again for all the treasures of the world.[30]

Unfortunately for Emily, the entrance exams were not the only tests the new students faced. Mary Lyon was concerned not only with the academic standing of her students, but with their spiritual state as well. Soon after the fall term began, Lyon questioned the new students to find out where they stood in their religious progress. This religious survey, and others like it taken throughout the year, forced a crisis in young Emily's life.

The Converting Ordinance

Like Emily's father and grandfather, Mary Lyon belonged to a Protestant sect known as the Congregationalists. Descended from the Puritans, who had simplified the beliefs of the Church of England, the Congregationalists believed that a person could attain eternal life by publicly confessing his or her faith in God. Solomon Stoddard, the leader of the Congregationalists in the Connecticut Valley in the late 1600s and early 1700s, called the doctrine of public confession the "converting ordinance."[31]

Emily's aunt Lavinia Norcross made such a confession in 1829, one year before Emily was born. "Yes the convert has enjoyment the world knows not of," she wrote. "I enjoy my mind very much & thought yesterday I was perfectly happy[;] my enjoyment does not consist in the fleeting pleasures of this world but it consists in a

"I Had a Great Mind to Be Homesick"

Emily Dickinson's brother, Austin, visited her at Mount Holyoke Female Seminary, bringing the homesick student a bounty of foodstuffs from home. Soon after, she wrote the following letter to Austin. Dickinson opens her letter, published in The Letters of Emily Dickinson, *with thanks for the treats, which she shared with her roommate, her cousin Emily.*

"Mt Holyoke. Seminary. Novr 6. 1847.

My dear Brother. Austin.

I have not really a moment of time in which to write you & am taking time from 'silent study hours,' but I am determined not to break my promise again & I generally carry my resolutions into effect. I watched you until you were out of sight Saturday evening & then went to my room & looked over my treasures & surely no miser ever counted his heaps of gold, with more satisfaction than I gazed upon the presents from home.

The cake, gingerbread, pie, & peaches are all devoured, but the—apples—chestnuts & grapes still remain & will I hope for some time. You may laugh if you want to, in view of the little time in which so many of the good things have disappeared but you must recollect that there are two instead of one to be fed & we have keen appetites over here. I cant tell you how much good your visit did me. My cough is almost gone & my spirits have wonderfully lightened since then. I had a great mind to be homesick after you went home, but I concluded not to, & therefore gave up all homesick feelings. Was not that a wise determination? . . .

Tell mother, that she was very thoughtful to inquire in regard to the welfare of my shoes. Emily has a shoe brush & plenty of blacking & I brush my shoes to my heart's content. Thank Viny 10,000. times for the beautiful ribbon & tell her to write me soon. Tell father I thank him for his letter & will try to follow its precepts. Do excuse the writing for I am in furious haste & cant write another word.

Your aff. Emily "

William Austin Dickinson, 1850.

perfect submission to the will of God. . . ."[32] Lavinia Norcross encouraged her sister, Emily's mother, to join her in the faith. A few months after Emily was born, Emily Norcross Dickinson converted.

Emily's father, however, did not confess his faith for another twenty years. According to a family friend, George Gould, Edward Dickinson found it hard to humble himself as required by the faith. "While Hon. E. D. of Amherst was converted," wrote Gould, "his pastor said to him in his study—'You want to come to Christ as a *lawyer*—but you must come to him as a *poor sinner*—get down on your knees & let me pray for you, & then you pray for yourself.'"[33] At last, Edward Dickinson confessed his faith. Perhaps to remind himself of this fateful day, Edward Dickinson carried a card in his wallet inscribed with the words "I hereby give myself to God"[34] and the date of his conversion.

The survey that Mary Lyon took in October 1847 was designed to find out how many of the new students had experienced such a conversion. Based on the answers she received, Mary Lyon placed each student in one of three categories. Those who had confessed their faith were known as "professors of faith." Those who seemed close to doing so were known as "hopers." Those who showed little desire to convert were termed "no-hopers." Most of the students took this public soul-searching seriously. In the October 2, 1847, entry to the Mount Holyoke Journal Letter—a diary kept by the faculty of the school— Susan L. Tolman noted:

> The names of the professors of religion, those who have a hope, and those who have not were taken. I cannot tell you how solemn it was, as one after another

class arose. I saw more than one weep as her name was put down *no hope*. There is a large class of this character[;] will it be so at the end of the year?[35]

Inner Conflicts

Emily Dickinson was not among the professors of faith. Although she believed in God and had attended church with her family throughout her girlhood, she had never confessed her faith in public. Like her father, she took the matter quite seriously. Her letters show that she had struggled with the issue for at least a year before her arrival at Mount Holyoke. Her close friend Abiah Root had converted in 1846. In letter after letter, Abiah urged Emily to follow her into the Congregationalist faith. Emily's reply, written on September 8, 1846, reveals both her reason for hesitating and the anguish her decision caused her:

> I am not unconcerned Dear A. upon the all important subject, to which you have so frequently & so affectionately called my attention in your letters. But I feel I have not yet made my peace with God. I am still a s[tran]ger—to the delightful emotions which fill your heart. I have perfect confidence in God & his promises & yet I know not why, I feel that the world holds a predominant place in my affections. I do not feel that I could give up all for Christ, were I called to die. Pray for me Dear A. that I may yet enter into the kingdom, that there may be room left for me in the shining courts above.[36]

The Congregationalist tradition required converts to renounce earthly life in order to attain a place in heaven. Emily loved the world too much to renounce it. To her, the world was a holy place. Her Christian schooling had taught her that every speck of the universe was God's creation and that His spirit was present in all of it. Why, then, she wondered, must she renounce the visible part of it? How could a person give up the known beauties of this world for the unknown glories of the next? Before her arrival at Mount Holyoke and throughout the year she spent there, Emily was tortured by questions like these.

In her afternoon lectures, Mary Lyon discussed the rewards of conversion and warned of the dangers of turning away from God. Likewise, the Sunday church sermons focused on issues of salvation. Mary Lyon also organized evening prayer meetings for the students who had not yet professed their faith. The pressure to convert was immense.

In December, Emily's cousin and roommate at Mount Holyoke, Emily Norcross, converted. Emily Norcross encouraged her cousin to convert as well. Weeks passed without any change, however. On January 11, 1848, Emily Norcross wrote to her family, "Emily Dickinson appears no different. I hoped I might have good news to write with regard to her."[37] A few days later, Emily Dickinson wrote to Abiah Root, "There is a great deal of religious interest here and many are flocking to the ark of safety." She was not among them, however. "I have not yet given up to the claims of Christ, but I trust I am not entirely thoughtless on so important & serious a subject,"[38] she confided.

Emily went home between semesters with the pressures of religious conversion very much on her mind. During vacation, she shared her concerns with her friend Abby Wood. In a letter to Abiah Root, Emily described her conversation with Abby about conversion.

> I had quite a long talk with Abby while at home and I doubt not she will soon cast her burden on Christ. She is sober, and keenly sensitive on the subject, and she says she only desires to be good. How I wish I could say that with sincerity, but I fear I never can.[39]

Always a keen observer of human behavior, Emily could see a rift forming between her and her friends. Their spiritual path and hers were not the same. What is more, she sensed they might never be. Emily did not want to lose Abiah or Abby as friends, however. To preserve the

Based on a daguerreotype taken at Mount Holyoke, this portrait of Emily Dickinson was created after the poet's death at the request of her family, who desired a more accurate image of the young woman they had known.

friendships, she decided to "no longer impose" her feelings upon them.[40]

Back to Amherst

In May, Emily returned home with no plans to return to Mount Holyoke. "Father has decided not to send me to Holyoke another year, so this is my *last term*,"[41] she wrote to Abiah on May 16, 1848. Emily ended the school year without confessing her faith. She left Mount Holyoke a "nohoper" in the eyes of Mary Lyon, her teachers, her classmates, and even herself.

Emily felt she had squandered a once-in-a-lifetime opportunity to become a

---

"Pining for a Valentine"

In February 1848, Emily Dickinson wrote to her brother from Mount Holyoke Female Seminary. At one point in the letter, number 22 of The Letters of Emily Dickinson, *Emily asked if any valentines had been sent to her.*

"I suppose you have written a few & received a quantity of Valentines this week. Every night I have looked & yet in vain for one of Cupid's messengers. Many of the girls have received very beautiful ones & I have not quite done hoping for one. Surely *my friend* THOMAS, has not lost all his former affection for me. I entreat you to tell him I am pining for a Valentine. I am sure I shall not very soon forget last Valentine week nor any the sooner, the fun I had at that time. Probably, Mary, Abby & Viny have received scores of them from the infatuated wights in the neighborhood while your *highly accomplished & gifted elder sister* is entirely overlooked. Monday afternoon, *Mistress* Lyon arose in the hall & forbade our sending 'any of those foolish notes called Valentines.' But those who were here last year, knowing her opinions, were sufficiently cunning to write & give them into the care of Dickinson, during vacation, so that about 150. were despatched on Valentine morn, before orders should be put down to the contrary effect. Hearing of this act, Miss Whitman by & with the advice & consent of the other teachers, with frowning brow, sallied over to the Post Office, to ascertain if possible, the number of Valentines and worse still, the names of the offenders. Nothing has yet been heard as to the amount of her information, but as Dickinson is a good hand to help the girls & no one has yet received sentence, we begin to think her mission unsuccessful. I have not written one nor do I now intend to."

Abiah Root (pictured here circa 1847) remained one of Emily's closest friends despite the fact that the two young women differed on religious matters.

I have neglected the *one needful thing* when all were obtaining it, and I may never, never again pass through such a season as was granted us last winter. Abiah, you may be surprised to hear me speak as I do, knowing that I express no interest in the all-important subject, but I am not happy, and I regret that last term, when that golden opportunity was mine, that I did not give up and become a Christian. It is not now too late, so my friends tell me, so my offended conscience whispers, but it is hard for me to give up the world.[42]

Emily Dickinson enrolled in Mount Holyoke hoping to further her education. No doubt her studies of physiology, chemistry, grammar, rhetoric, history, and botany enlarged her understanding of the world. But the greatest lesson she learned was about herself. As she watched classmate after classmate declare themselves for Jesus, she realized how different she was from her friends. She did not share their faith, and she sensed she never would. Still, she believed the world to be a holy place. She knew she could not belong in the church of her peers, but this did not mean her quest for spiritual enlightenment had come to an end. On the contrary, it had barely begun.

Christian. Her regret was tempered by one inescapable fact, however. She knew that she was not yet ready to renounce the world she loved. In her letter to Abiah, she reflected on her failure to convert. Her anguish is palpable, but so is her honesty:

3 A Friend Who Taught Immortality

Emily Dickinson's return to Amherst in May 1848 brought relief from the pressures she had endured at Mount Holyoke, but not from the questions in her mind. She continued to seek answers about life, death, and the afterlife in the books she read and in the conversations she had with friends and family. At this time of spiritual searching, Emily Dickinson met someone who would change her life forever. His name was Ben Newton.

Nine years older than Emily Dickinson, Ben Newton grew up in nearby Worcester, Massachusetts. Late in 1847, while Emily was away at Mount Holyoke, Newton traveled to Amherst to study law with Edward Dickinson. Emily may have met Newton in February 1848, during the break between semesters. If not, she certainly made his acquaintance when she returned from Mount Holyoke in May.

A Faith in Things Unseen

Edward Dickinson often invited his law students into his home, and Ben Newton was no exception. No record exists of how many visits Newton made to the Dickinson home, nor when he and Emily first met. Still, a letter Emily wrote to the pastor of Newton's church several years later describes the unique bond that formed between them:

> I was then but a child, yet I was old enough to admire the strength, and grace, of an intellect far surpassing my own, and it taught me many lessons. . . . Mr. Newton became to me a gentle yet grave Preceptor, teaching me what to read, what authors to admire, and what was most grand or beautiful in nature, and that sublimer lesson, a faith in things unseen, and in a life again, nobler, and much more blessed.[43]

Newton belonged to the Unitarian Church, a faith very different from the one Emily had grown up in. The name Unitarian is derived from the Latin word *unitarius*. It means "of or pertaining to a unit or whole." The Unitarians believe God exists as a single unit. They differ in this regard from the Congregationalists and most other Christians, who believe God exists in three equal parts, or a trinity. Trinitarians revere God the Father, God the Son, and God the Holy Ghost—with Jesus being the Son. Since Unitarians believe in just one God, they do not find it necessary to confess their faith in Jesus. Indeed, many Unitarians do not consider themselves Christians at all.

As Dickinson's letter to his pastor suggests, Newton shared his Unitarian beliefs with her. Newton's words intrigued Dickinson. For the first time she began to see that it might be possible to reject the Congregationalist faith without rejecting God—or being rejected by Him. Emily Dickinson never joined the Unitarian Church, and her struggles with the Christian faith continued throughout her life. Still, her contact with the Unitarian beliefs gave her an inner peace that she had never before known. "When I was a little Girl, I had a friend, who taught me Immortality,"[44] Emily Dickinson wrote many years later, referring to the conversations she and Newton had about the afterlife. Ben Newton gave her hope that even non-Christians might experience some kind of eternal life.

He also gave her books. An avid reader, Newton loaned Emily and Lavinia the works of Lydia Maria Child, the Brontë sisters, and others. In 1850, after Newton passed the bar exam, he moved back to Worcester. From there he sent Emily her cherished copy of Emerson's *Poems*. In letters she wrote later, Dickinson referred to Newton as her "tutor" and her "preceptor." No details survive about the discussions the two young people had about books and authors. Dickinson's description of Newton as "an intellect far surpassing my

This daguerreotype of Emily Dickinson, taken in late 1847 or early 1848, is the only surviving, authenticated photograph of the famous poet.

First Publication

The Indicator, *a periodical published by students of Amherst College, printed an anonymous Valentine letter in the February 7, 1850, issue. The letter, which appeared in a column edited by Henry Shipley entitled "Editor's Corner," is here excerpted from* The Letters of Emily Dickinson. *"I wish I knew who the author is,"* Shipley *wrote, introducing the letter. "I think she must have some spell, by which she quickens the imagination, and causes the high blood 'run frolic through the veins.'"* The author of the Valentine letter was Emily Dickinson.

"Valentine Eve

Magnum bonum, 'harum scarum,' zounds et zounds, et war alarum, man reformam, life perfectum, mundum changum, all things flarum?

Sir, I desire an interview; meet me at sunrise, or sunset, or the new moon—the place is immaterial. In gold, or in purple, or sackcloth—I look not upon *raiment*. With sword, or with pen, or with plough—the weapons are less than the *wielder*. In coach, or in wagon, or walking, the *equipage* far from the *man*. With soul, or spirit, or body, they are all alike to me. With host or alone, in sunshine or storm, in heaven or earth, *some* how or *no* how—I propose, sir, to see you.

And not to *see* merely, but a chat, sir, or a tete-a-tete, a confab, a mingling of opposite minds is what I propose to have. I feel sir that we shall agree. . . . We will talk over what we have learned in our geographies, and listened to from the pulpit, the press and the Sabbath School.

This is strong language sir, but none the less true. So hurrah for North Carolina, since we are on this point.

Our friendship sir, shall endure till sun and moon shall wane no more, till stars shall set, and victims rise to grace the final sacrifice. We'll be instant, in season, out of season, minister, take care of, cherish, sooth, watch, wait, doubt, refrain, reform, elevate, instruct. . . .

But the world is sleeping in ignorance and error, sir, and we must be crowing cocks, and singing larks, and a rising sun to awake her; or else we'll pull society up to the roots, and plant it in a different place. We'll build Alms-houses, and transcendental State prisons, and scaffolds—we will blow out the sun, and the moon, and encourage invention. Alpha shall kiss Omega—we will ride up the hill of glory—Hallelujah, all hail!

Yours, truly,
C."

own"[45] suggests that the law student must have had worthwhile things to say about the literature of the time.

Encouragement

One more, very important fact suggests that Ben Newton possessed uncommon insight about writers and writing. He encouraged Emily Dickinson to be a poet. No record exists of exactly when or how this occurred, either, but there can be no doubt that it did. Many years later, after Newton had died, Dickinson recalled, "My dying Tutor told me he would like to live till I had been a poet."[46] Dickinson's earliest surviving poem dates from the time that Ben Newton lived in Amherst.

In February 1850, Dickinson sent a Valentine's Day poem to her father's law partner, Elbridge Bowdoin. Ten years older than Emily, Bowdoin had visited her at Mount Holyoke Seminary and had loaned her a copy of Emily Brontë's novel *Jane Eyre*. The poem provides more than a glimmer of the talent she possessed. It begins conventionally enough: "Oh the Earth was *made* for lovers, for damsel, and hopeless swain."[47] The next few lines describe other traditional couples, such as a bride and a bridegroom and Adam and Eve. The poem then spirals outward to include various pairings from nature: a bee and a flower; the wind and branches; a storm and the shore; a wave and the moon; night and day; morning and evening; earth and heaven. These images fit with Dickinson's theme that "Earth was made for lovers," but the pairings are imaginative and fresh. Even more impressive is the ease and speed with which the poem's focus expands. Some-

times reading a poem by Emily Dickinson is like looking through a kaleidoscope. The poem starts with one scene, then quickly and precisely shifts to another, then to another, and to another, each time offering a new and unique view of the world. Her 1850 Valentine poem works like this.

Dickinson's first poem contains one especially striking and characteristic image. Line twenty-one reads, "The worm doth woo [court] the mortal, death claims a living bride."[48] Dickinson's use of an image of death in the middle of a Valentine poem might seem strange, but the line is neither jarring nor grotesque. Young as she was, Dickinson controlled the poem in a way that made the image fit. By the time the line appears, Dickinson has made it clear that the poem is not just about human beings, but all of nature. Death is part of the natural world, Dickinson reminds the reader. It is an essential part of life itself. Over the next thirty-six years, Emily Dickinson returned to this theme hundreds of times in her work.

A Published Poem

It is possible that Ben Newton saw this poem. After all, he worked in the same law office as Bowdoin, and his relationship with Dickinson was at its peak in 1850. Newton almost certainly saw a Valentine poem written two years later, which Dickinson gave to another of her father's law partners, William Howland. On February 20, 1852, when Dickinson was twenty-one, the Springfield *Daily Republican* published the sixty-eight-line poem under the title "A Valentine." It was Emily Dickinson's first published poem.

While the 1850 Valentine poem contains quite a few serious passages, the 1852 poem is a lark. It shows Dickinson at her high-spirited best. The poet offers the poem to an unnamed young man as a "momento mori," or keepsake, to remind him of her when they are separated. Like the earlier Valentine poem, the 1852 poem includes a variety of images. This time, the effect is light-hearted rather than grave:

> Hurrah for Peter Parley!
>   Hurrah for Daniel Boone!
> Three cheers, sir, for the gentleman
>   Who first observed the moon!
>
> Peter, put up the sunshine;
>   Patti, arrange the stars;
> Tell Luna, *tea* is waiting,
>   And call your brother Mars!

Only toward the end of the poem does the tone become more serious:

> In token of our friendship
>   Accept this "Bonnie Doon,"
> And when the hand that plucked it
>   Hath passed beyond the moon,
>
> The memory of my ashes
>   Will consolation be;
> Then, farewell, Tuscarora,
>   And farewell, Sir, to thee![49]

By the time the poem appeared, Newton was living in Worcester. No letter survives to prove that Newton saw the poem, although Dickinson later wrote that she and Newton kept their friendship alive despite the distance between them. "During his life in Worcester, he often wrote to me, and I replied to his letters,"[50] Dickinson wrote a few months after Newton died. While William Howland no doubt valued the poem as the token of friendship it was meant to be, he probably did not appreciate the poetry in it as much as the young man living in Worcester who "had hoped to live till [she] had been a poet."[51]

Ben Newton was diagnosed with consumption (pulmonary tuberculosis) shortly after he left Amherst. He informed Dickinson of his illness by letter. Clearly, he missed Emily and the times they had spent together. Dickinson later recalled, "My earliest friend wrote me the week before he died 'If I live, I will go to Amherst. If I die, I certainly will.'"[52]

Newton must have spared his friend some of the details about his illness, because his death in March 1853 shocked Dickinson. She wrote to her brother, "Monday noon. Oh Austin, Newton is dead. The first of my own friends."[53] Ben Newton was not the first person Dickinson knew well who had died, so it was a measure of their closeness that she referred to him as "the first" of her "own friends" to do so.

Spiritual Questions

Newton's death not only broke Emily Dickinson's heart, but it also raised questions in her mind—the same questions that had vexed her since Mount Holyoke. Newton had taught her that a person could love God without accepting Jesus as a savior. This belief had given Dickinson hope, but it went against the teachings of the Congregational Church. The Unitarian ideas were so different from those of her family, her teachers, and her friends that Dickinson still wondered if they could be true. Two things were at stake. One was Ben Newton's fate after death—whether his soul went to heaven or hell. The other was Dickinson's own fate, were she to follow in his footsteps.

Review of a Concert

On July 4, 1851, the world-famous soprano Jenny Lind gave a concert at Edwards Church in Amherst. All of the Dickinsons except Austin attended the performance. In letter number 46 of The Letters of Emily Dickinson, *Dickinson described the concert for her brother, who was in Boston at the time.*

"We all loved Jenny Lind, but not accustomed oft to her manner of singing did'nt fancy *that* so well as we did *her*—no doubt it was very fine—but take some notes from her 'Echo'—the bird sounds from the 'Bird Song' and some of her curious trills, and I'd rather have a Yankee.

Herself, and not her music, was what we seemed to love—she had an air of *exile* in her mild blue eyes, and a something sweet and touching in her native accent which charms her many friends— 'Give me my thatched cottage' as she sang grew so earnest she seemed half lost in song and for a transient time I fancied she *had* found it and would be seen 'na mair,' and then her foreign accent made her again a wanderer—we will talk about her sometime when you come— Father sat all the evening looking *mad,* and *silly,* and yet so much amused that you would have *died* a laughing—when the performers bowed, he said 'Good evening Sir'—and when they retired, 'very well—that will do,' it was'nt *sarcasm* exactly, nor it was'nt *disdain,* it was infinitely funnier than either of those virtues, as if old Abraham had come to see the show, and thought it was all very well, but a little excess of *Monkey!*"

The soprano Jenny Lind was known around the world as "The Swedish Nightingale" because of her clear, high, fluid voice.

Dickinson pondered these matters for months. Finally, she wrote to the pastor of Newton's church, Edward Everett Hale, to inquire about her friend's "last hours." She reasoned that if Newton's beliefs about God had merit, he would have greeted death "cheerfully." If they did not, perhaps he would have realized it on his deathbed and expressed some regrets.

I think, Sir, you were the Pastor of Mr B. F. Newton, who died sometime since in Worcester, and I often have hoped to know if his last hours were cheerful, and if he was willing to die. . . . You may think my desire strange, Sir, but the Dead was dear to me, and I would love to know that he sleeps peacefully. . . . During his life in Worcester, he often wrote to

News of a Fire

In letter 49 of The Letters of Emily Dickinson, *Emily described to Austin how a fire tore through part of Amherst in July 1851. Despite the seriousness of the situation, Dickinson as usual found room in the story for a little comic relief.*

"*Yesterday* there was a *fire*—at about 3. in the afternoon Mr Kimberly's barn was discovered to be on fire—the wind was blowing a gale directly from the west, and having had no rain, the roofs [were] as dry as stubble. Mr Palmer's house was cleared—the *little house* of Father's, and Mr Kimberly's also. The engine was broken and it seemed for a little while as if the whole street must go. The Kimberly barn was burnt down, and the house much charred and injured, tho not at all destroyed. Mr Palmer's barn took fire and Dea Leland's, also, but were extinguised with only part burned roofs. We all feel very thankful at such a narrow escape. Father says there was never such imminent danger, and such miraculous escape. Father and Mr Frink took charge of the fire, or rather of the *water*, since fire *usually* takes care of *itself*. The men all worked like heroes, and after the fire was out Father gave commands to have them march to Howe's where an entertainment was provided for them—after the whole was over, they gave 'three cheers for Edward Dickinson, and three more for the Insurance Company'!

On the whole it is very wonderful that we did'nt all burn up, and we ought to hold our tongues and be very thankful. If there *must be* a fire I'm sorry it couldnt wait until you had got home, because you seem to enjoy such things so very much."

me, and I replied to his letters— I always asked for his health, and he answered so cheerfully, that while I knew he was ill, his death indeed surprised me. He often talked of God, but I do not know certainly if he was his Father in Heaven— Please Sir, to tell me if he was willing to die, and if you think him at Home, I should love so much to know certainly, that he was today in Heaven.[54]

Hale's reply has not survived, but he probably assured Dickinson that her friend was indeed "at Home" with God. It is scarcely imaginable that a pastor of the Unitarian Church would have replied otherwise. Whatever Hale's reply, it did not remove the nagging doubts from Dickinson's mind. She continued to search for answers to the mysteries of God, death, and the afterlife.

One of those she turned to in her spiritual quest was Reverend Charles Wadsworth. Wadsworth served as the pastor of the Arch Street Presbyterian Church in Philadelphia. She saw and possibly met Wadsworth in 1854. One and a half years earlier, Dickinson's father had been elected to the U.S. House of Representatives. The family decided to visit Representative Dickinson in Washington in April 1854. From the nation's capital, Emily and Lavinia traveled to Philadelphia to visit the family of Eliza Coleman, an old friend from Amherst. Emily probably went with the Colemans to hear Wadsworth preach.

After she returned to Amherst, Emily Dickinson wrote to Wadsworth. Her letters to him have not survived, but one of his letters was found among Dickinson's papers after she died. Wadsworth did not date the letter, but he did spell Dickinson's name wrong. This mistake prompted Cynthia Griffin Wolff, a Dickinson biographer,

The Reverend Charles Wadsworth was a Presbyterian minister famous for his preaching skills.

to conclude that the note was probably "a very early letter, possibly even the first, given that he misspells her name."[55]

In his letter, Wadsworth answers a note he received from Dickinson—a letter that clearly upset him. "I am distressed beyond measure at your note, received this moment,"[56] he wrote. Wadsworth's letter is only three sentences long. In that short space he referred to Dickinson's "affliction," "trial," and "sorrow." Clearly Dickinson impressed him as troubled. If, as Wolff and other scholars believe, Dickinson wrote to Wadsworth shortly after her visit to Philadelphia, then she must have composed the letter soon after writing to Edward Everett Hale. The "sorrow" she mentioned to Wadsworth likely was the same as the one she described to Hale. She was still mourning the loss of Ben Newton. She probably hoped that Wadsworth could comfort her about her friend's death.

"*I Am One of the Lingering Bad Ones*"

In 1850 Amherst was the scene of a religious revival. Emily's father and many of her friends, including her old schoolmate Abby Wood, converted to the faith. The revival caused Emily to reflect on her religious state in a letter to Abiah Root, number 36 in The Letters of Dickinson.

"I presume you have heard from Abby, and know what she now believes—she makes a sweet, girl christian, religion makes her face quite different, calmer, but full of radiance, holy, yet very joyful. She talks of herself quite freely, seems to love Lord Christ most dearly, and to wonder, and be bewildered, at the life she has always led. It all looks black, and distant, and God, and Heaven are near, she is certainly much changed.

She has told you about things here, how the 'still small voice' is calling, and how people are listening, and believing, and truly obeying—how the place is very solemn, and sacred, and the bad ones slink away, and are sorrowful—not at their wicked lives—but at this strange time, great change. *I* am one of the lingering *bad* ones, and so do *I* slink away, and pause and ponder, and ponder and pause, and do work without knowing why, not surely, for *this* brief world, and more sure it is not for Heaven—and I ask what this message *means* that they ask for so very eagerly; *you* know this depth, and fulness, will you *try* to tell me about it."

Wadsworth replied to Dickinson's letters, but apparently not at the depth she craved. Years later, in the same letter in which Dickinson described Ben Newton as the friend who taught her immortality, Dickinson wrote, "Then I found one more—but he was not contented I be his scholar. . . ." Wadsworth could not, or would not, help her. Dickinson was on her own. Recalling this time, she later wrote, "Soon after, my Tutor, died—and for several years, my Lexicon [dictionary]—was my only companion."[57]

Haunted by the losses in her life, vexed by religious doubts, and awed to the point of terror by the workings of nature, Emily Dickinson began to write poetry. "I sing, as the Boy does by the Burying Ground—because I am afraid," she later explained. The process of writing brought Emily Dickinson comfort. "When . . . a sudden light on Orchards, or a new fashion in the wind troubled my attention—I felt a palsy, here—the Verses just relieve."[58]

Throughout her life, Emily Dickinson would continue to be disturbed by unusual thoughts, feelings, and visions. Around the age of twenty-five, however, she found that writing poetry helped her cope with the mysteries of her world. It was a discovery that eventually would enrich the lives of millions.

Chapter

4 Poet

As the daughter of a well-to-do lawyer, Emily Dickinson was not expected to find a career or support herself. Most women in her position married men of similar class and did not have to work for a living. This is not to say that Dickinson did no work at all. Along with her sister and mother, she performed many household duties, including baking, gardening, and sewing. "Em is an excellent housekeeper," observed Joseph Lyman, who visited the Dickinson home many times as a young man and later wrote a popular book entitled *The Philosophy of Housekeeping.* Emily and Lavinia learned many of their domestic skills from their mother. "Vinnie's mother was a rare and delicate cook in such matters as crullers and custards and she taught the girls all those housewifely accomplishments,"[59] Lyman added.

Emily was especially known for her baking. When she was twenty-five, she won second prize in the 1856 Cattle Show for her rye and Indian bread. The next year, she served on the committee that judged the contest. Her father, Emily once remarked to a friend, liked only her bread, so she did most of the family's baking.[60]

Dickinson did not like cleaning, however, referring to it as "a prickly art."[61] She helped with many other chores, however. In a letter to her cousin, she described the small tasks she performed as she recovered from a treatment for her eyes:

> For the first few weeks I did nothing but comfort my plants, till now their small green cheeks are covered with smiles. I chop the chicken centres when we have roast fowl, frequent now.

Lavinia Norcross Dickinson, from a picture taken about 1852. Vinnie shared household duties with her mother and her elder sister.

. . . Then I make the yellow to the pies, and bang the spice for cake, and knit the soles to the stockings I knit the bodies to last June. They say I am a "help." Partly because it is true, I suppose, and the rest applause.[62]

While Emily, her sister, and her mother performed most of the routine chores around the house, the heavier work—cleaning, laundry, tending to the stable, and the like—was left for the servants the Dickinsons employed. As a result, Emily Dickinson had time to pursue the one thing that brought her a measure of peace: poetry.

A Growing Occupation

Between 1855 and 1858, Dickinson came to see herself as a poet. Because she rarely dated her poems, it is difficult to tell exactly when she composed them. Thomas H. Johnson, who edited the first complete collection of Dickinson's poems in 1955, arranged the poems in what he believed to be their order of composition. He assigned each poem a probable date. Johnson based these dates on an analysis of Dickinson's handwriting. He compared the handwriting of poems to the handwriting of letters, most of which are dated. Based on this evidence, Johnson concluded that Dickinson wrote at least fifty-one poems between 1855 and 1858.

Johnson believes that 1858 was the year in which Dickinson created the first of forty-nine "volumes . . . tied together with twine," as her sister, Lavinia, later described the small packets of poetry Dickinson assembled throughout her life. In his introduction to *The Complete Poems of Emily*

Dickinson, Johnson described when and how Dickinson made her packets:

> Meanwhile, probably in 1858, she winnowed her earlier verses, transcribing those she chose to save into the earliest of the famous packets. Always in ink, the packets are gatherings of four, five, or six sheets of folded stationery loosely held together by thread looped through them in the spine, at two points equidistant from the top and bottom.[63]

By 1858 Dickinson apparently believed she had written poems worth keeping. Among the fifty-one poems she copied into her first packet are several fine ones and two or three that many critics rank among her best. The following poem is one of the latter.

Emily Dickinson as depicted by Barry Moser. Around 1858, Dickinson began to copy her poems into small packets.

I never lost as much but twice,
And that was in the sod.
Twice have I stood a beggar
Before the door of God!

Angels—twice descending
Reimbursed my store—
Burglar! Banker—Father!
I am poor once more![64]

The speaker in this poem expresses grief and anger at the death of two people close to her. This anger is directed toward God, who has twice sent angels to claim the souls of loved ones. The speaker not only refers to God as "Father," the traditional image of God, but also as a "Banker" and a "Burglar." As a banker, God has the power to keep account of human lives. As a burglar, he can enter a home and whisk away a human soul. Neither image is very flattering toward the creator of the universe. In just eight lines, the poem precisely portrays the helplessness and resentment the speaker feels before an all-powerful God.

All poems reflect the thoughts and feelings of the people who compose them, of course, but the words of a poem cannot always be taken as the literal beliefs of its author. A poet may include certain words or arrange them in a particular way to create a desired effect. Poets often exaggerate events or even invent them to make better poems. For this reason, readers of poetry must be careful not to assume that the thoughts expressed by the "speaker" of the poem and the beliefs of the poet are the same thing. That is not to say, however, that poets never express their deepest beliefs in their poems. They often do. It is especially hard for a reader of Emily Dickinson's work to separate the speaker of the verse from the poet herself. Dickinson was more than willing to

The manuscript of Dickinson's poem, "They shut Me up in Prose." Thomas H. Johnson assigned dates to Dickinson's poems based on his analysis of her handwriting.

"tell all the Truth but tell it slant," as she once put it, to create a more powerful work. "When I state myself, as the Representative of the Verse—it does not mean—me—but a supposed person,"[65] she once explained.

At the same time, Dickinson clearly based many of her poems on real events in her life, and her words often come across as honest and sincere. Dickinson probably composed "I never lost as much but twice" to express the anger and loss she felt at the death of Ben Newton and another friend, probably Sophia Holland. Thomas Johnson suggests that Leonard Humphrey, a teacher at Amherst Academy who died in

"A Fairy Morning"

A three-day snowstorm hit Amherst right after the New Year in 1859. During the storm, Emily Dickinson took a moment to write a letter, number 199 in The Letters of Emily Dickinson, *to her cousin Louise Norcross. Dickinson playfully hints at her ambitions to be "great" by learning to "sing."*

"Since it snows this morning, dear Loo, too fast for interruption, put your brown curls in a basket, and come sit with me.

I am sewing for Vinnie, and Vinnie is flying through the flakes to buy herself a little hood. It's quite a fairy morning, and I often lay down my needle, and 'build a castle in the air' which seriously impedes the sewing project. What if I pause a little longer, and write a note to you! Who will be the wiser? I have known little of you, since the October morning when our families went out driving, and you and I in the dining-room decided to be distinguished. It's a great thing to be 'great,' Loo, and you and I might tug for a life, and never accomplish it, but no one can stop our looking on, and you know some cannot sing, but the orchard is full of birds, and we all can listen. What if we learn, ourselves, some day! Who indeed knows?"

1850, was the other loss Dickinson referred to in the poem. This seems unlikely. In her 1846 letter to Abiah Root, Dickinson introduced the story of Sophia Holland's death by stating, "I never lost but one friend"[66]—words clearly echoed in "I never lost as much but twice." In addition, Dickinson wrote that Sophia Holland's death sent her into a period of "fixed melancholy," something she never said about Humphrey's death. Regardless of its biographical origins, the poem stands as a stark and memorable account of loss.

The 1858 packet contains another poem that calls to mind the death of the man who gave her "a faith in things unseen, and in a life again, nobler, and much more blessed":[67]

Adrift! A little boat adrift!
And night is coming down!
Will *no* one guide a little boat
Unto the nearest town?

So Sailors say—on yesterday—
Just as the dusk was brown
One little boat gave up its strife
And gurgled down and down.

So angels say—on yesterday—
Just as the dawn was red
One little boat—o'erspent with gales—
Retrimmed its masts—redecked its
sails—
And shot—exultant on![68]

In just thirteen lines, Dickinson offers three different views of the same event— the sinking of a boat. The first account comes from the speaker of the poem, who watches as the boat drifts on the sea before the coming night. The speaker draws attention to the plight of the boat and pleads for help. The second account comes from "Sailors." They report that the boat sank at dusk. The third version comes from angels. From their angle, the boat did not sink at sunset. Rather, it survived the gales and "shot—exultant on" at dawn.

In this poem, Dickinson contrasts an earthly view of things with a heavenly view. The view from earth is limited; it appears that death is the end. If human beings could see things as the angels do, Dickinson suggests, they would know that this is an illusion. Death is not the end, but a change—a new beginning. The boat was not lost. It continued on its journey into the afterlife.

Contrasts and Contradictions

Written at two different times, in two different moods, "I never lost as much but twice" and "Adrift! A little boat adrift" offer contrasting views of God, death, and eternity. "I never lost as much but twice" portrays God as a burglar and offers little hope of life after death. "Adrift! A little boat adrift" suggests that while God may appear indifferent to the plight of human beings, in the end He provides them with an afterlife.

These are not the only poems Dickinson wrote that seem to contradict one another. On the contrary, many of her poems seem at odds with each other. This is part of what makes Dickinson unique—and great. She did not impose limits on herself by forcing herself to be consistent. Just as

an individual poem by Emily Dickinson may work like a kaleidoscope, swiftly and precisely shifting scenes, so too does the entire body of her work. Dickinson gracefully moves from one point of view to another, offering a fresh perspective with each turn of her prismatic mind.

In 1859 Dickinson nearly doubled the poetic output of the previous five years, according to Thomas Johnson's count. He concluded that Dickinson wrote ninety-three poems in 1859—nearly two a week.[69] Day by day, the twenty-nine-year-old poet was growing more assured in her art. She began to include her poems in her letters to friends. In a letter written to Mary Emerson Haven in February 1859, for example, Dickinson added a four-line poem about the sadness of waking up and realizing that a loved one is far away, or perhaps dead:

> A darting fear—a pomp—a tear—
> A waking on a morn
> To find that what one waked for,
> Inhales the different dawn.[70]

Dickinson also began to enclose poems with gifts she gave. In 1859 she penned these lines, probably to accompany a bouquet of flowers from her garden:

> South Winds jostle them—
> Bumblebees come—
> Hover—hesitate—
> Drink, and are gone—
>
> Butterflies pause
> On their passage Cashmere—
> I—softly plucking,
> Present them here![71]

As her confidence in her skills grew, Dickinson began to experiment with rhythm, rhyme, and punctuation. In "South Winds jostle them," for example, she used a strict meter in all eight lines.

However, only two of the lines—the second and the fifth—are arranged in the same way. Few poets of the time would have dared to change the meter of the lines so many times in such a short poem. Dickinson did this kind of thing routinely.

A Singular Style

About this time, Dickinson also began to punctuate her poems with dashes. She placed dashes not only at the ends of lines, but within them. For example, lines three and six of "South Winds jostle them" contain such dashes. The dashes help control the rhythmic flow of the poems, but Dickinson was the first—and remains the only—well-known poet to use dashes in this way.

Another unique feature of Dickinson's poems was her use of capitalization. Increasingly, she capitalized not just proper nouns, but even common ones. In "South Winds jostle them," for example, she capitalized "Winds," even though it is not a proper noun. Such capitalization is not standard practice in English, but it is in German, which Dickinson studied at Amherst Academy. Since English speakers normally expect capital letters to denote names and other proper nouns, Dickinson's Germanlike capitalization has the odd effect of making common objects seem more important than usual, almost alive. A "robin" becomes a "Robin," as if the bird possessed a proper name. In this way, Dickinson subtly anthropomorphizes, or gives human traits to, plants, animals, and inanimate objects. In this poem about a spider, for example, Dickinson's capitalization confers humanlike qualities on not only

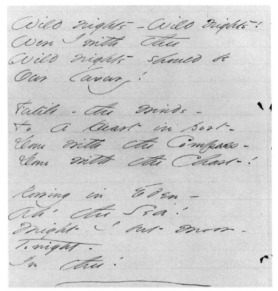

The manuscript of "Wild Nights—Wild Nights!" clearly shows the poet's unusual capitalization and punctuation.

the spider, but also on his web, a broom, and even "nought," or nothingness:

> The Spider holds a Silver Ball
> In unperceived Hands—
> And dancing softly to Himself
> His Yarn of Pearl—unwinds—
>
> He plies from Nought to Nought—
> In unsubstantial Trade—
> Supplants our Tapestries with His—
> In half the period—
>
> An Hour to rear supreme
> His Continents of Light—
> Then dangle from the Housewife's
>   Broom—
> His Boundaries—forgot—[72]

Through capitalization, Dickinson played another trick of the kaleidoscope: she made small things appear large and large things appear small. By capitalizing everyday objects, Dickinson focuses the reader's attention on them in a new way, making them appear large and important. By capitalizing large, abstract things, she gives them humanlike qualities, making them seem smaller, more familiar, and easier to understand.

Dickinson had an unusual ear for rhyme, and she had the courage to employ it in her work. For example, every even numbered line in "The Spider holds a Silver Ball" rhymes, but none of the pairings are perfect rhymes. Dickinson loved suspended rhymes—the same final consonant sound preceded by a different vowel sound. In "The Spider holds a Silver Ball," she used three suspended rhymes: "hands" and "unwinds," "trade" and "period," and "light" and "forgot."

Dickinson used many other kinds of imperfect rhymes as well. For example, in "There is a Languor of the Life," she rhymed "severe" with "there."[73] This is known as a spelled rhyme—two words that end with the same letters but have different sounds. Dickinson also employed open rhymes, two words that end with vowel sounds that do not sound alike.

Seeking an Audience

According to Thomas Johnson's count, Dickinson wrote sixty-three poems in 1860 and another eighty-five in 1861.[74] As she became more accomplished in the art of making poems, Dickinson began to seek an audience for her work. The person she turned to more than any other was her friend from her days at Amherst Academy, Susan Gilbert. In 1856 Sue married Austin Dickinson. This union brought Emily Dickinson both delight and despair—delight because it meant Susan would be part of her family, and despair because Emily

---

Finding Comfort in Words

This 1860 poem— which appeared in the Round Table *in 1864 under the title "My Sabbath," was included in* Poems, First Series, *and was published in this form in* The Poems of Emily Dickinson—*describes one possible resolution to the religious conflicts in Dickinson's life.*

Some keep the Sabbath going to Church—
I keep it, staying at Home—
With a Bobolink for a Chorister—
And an Orchard, for a Dome—

Some keep the Sabbath in Surplice—
I just wear my Wings—
And instead of tolling the Bell, for Church,
Our little Sexton—sings.

God preaches, a noted Clergyman—
And the sermon is never long,
So instead of getting to Heaven, at last—
I'm going, all along.

would have to compete with her brother for the attention of her beloved friend.

When Sue and Austin got married, Edward Dickinson gave them a parcel of land next to his own. The newlyweds built a home on the lot and lived next door to the Dickinson Homestead for the rest of Emily Dickinson's life. In those years, Emily Dickinson sent about three hundred poems across the hedge to her sister-in-law.

Like Emily, Susan Gilbert Dickinson had a taste for literature and the arts. In the same letter that Emily wrote to Sue about the arrival of Longfellow's *Golden Legend* at the local bookstore, Dickinson described Sue and herself as two people "who please ourselves with the fancy that we are the only poets, and everyone else is *prose*."[75]

In 1861 Emily sent Sue a draft of a poem that later became one of her most famous works:

Emily's friend, Susan Gilbert. Sue married Austin Dickinson in 1856. The newlyweds built a home next door to the Dickinson Homestead and lived there for the rest of Emily's life.

Safe in their Alabaster Chambers,
Untouched by Morning
And untouched by Noon—
Sleep the meek members of the
    Resurrection,
Rafter of satin
And Roof of stone.

Light laughs the breeze
In her Castle above them—
Babbles the Bee in stolid Ear,
Pipe the Sweet Birds in ignorant
    cadence—
Ah, what sagacity perished here![76]

This brief poem shows Dickinson at her most kaleidoscopic. The first stanza describes the world of the deceased. They lie in their coffins awaiting the moment when they will be raised from the dead in an event Christians refer to as the Resurrection. Several key words—alabaster, satin, stone—evoke coolness and motionlessness. In the second stanza, Dickinson shifts focus from the world below to the world above. Warmth, light, and sound flood into the poem. A breeze "laughs," a bee "babbles," and birds "pipe." Although separated by only a few feet of earth, the two worlds are vastly different; the power of the poem lies in the contrast between them.

Criticism

Sue's response to the poem has not survived, but she must have objected to the second stanza. Perhaps the shift in focus struck her as too abrupt. Whatever her complaint, Emily responded by sending her a draft of the poem that included a new second stanza. The new stanza still contrasts the world below with the world above. Dickinson replaced the scenes from nature with something more abstract, mathematical, and cool:

> Safe in their Alabaster Chambers—
> Untouched by Morning—
> And untouched by Noon—
> Lie the meek members of the
>   Resurrection—
> Rafter of Satin—and Roof of Stone!
>
> Grand go the Years—in the Crescent—
>   above them—
> Worlds scoop their Arcs—
> And Firmaments—row—
> Diadems—drop—and Doges—
>   surrender—
> Soundless as dots—on a Disc
>   of Snow—[77]

"Perhaps this verse will please you better—Sue—,"[78] Dickinson wrote at the bottom of the poem.

It did not. "I am not suited dear Emily with the second verse," Sue wrote back, immediately dashing any hopes Emily might have had of pleasing her friend. Using a high-flown simile, Sue first praised the new stanza. "It is remarkable as the chain lightening that blinds us hot nights in the Southern sky," she wrote. Then she added her objection, "but it does not go with the ghostly shimmer of the first verse as well as the other one."[79]

Like many readers, Sue found the first stanza to be stronger than either of the second stanzas. Sue carried her enthusiasm for the stanza too far, however, suggesting that it could stand alone as a complete poem. "It just occurs to me that the first verse is complete in itself and needs no other," Sue wrote. "Strange things always go alone." Sue then revealed her shortcomings, not only as a critic, but also as a friend. She dismissed Emily's efforts to

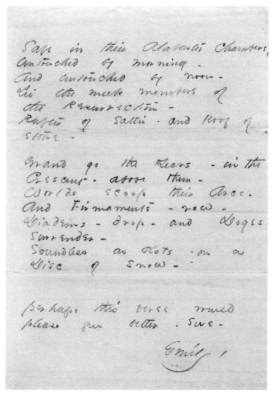

A manuscript of the second draft of "Safe in their Alabaster Chambers." At the bottom is Dickinson's note, "Perhaps this verse will please you better—Sue."

compose a complementary second stanza in a callous (not to mention shortsighted) way. "You never made a peer for that verse," Sue went on, "and I *guess* you[r] kingdom does'nt hold one."[80]

Sue's words may have stung Dickinson personally, but as a poet she brushed them aside. She knew that as well crafted as the first stanza is, it requires a second stanza for contrast. She rejected Sue's suggestion to let the first stanza stand alone. Instead, she sent her sister-in-law a third version of the second stanza. At the top, perhaps mockingly, Dickinson wrote, "Is *this frostier?*"

> Springs—shake the sills—
> But—the Echoes—stiffen—

Oar—is the Window—
And numb—the Door—
Tribes of Eclipse—in Tents of
    Marble—
Staples of Ages—have buckled—
    there—[81]

Even Dickinson could not surpass her second version for an air of frosty grandeur. Her third effort has a desperate tone to it, suggesting that she was exasperated by her sister-in-law's criticism. In a note that accompanied the stanza, the author of

A Message of Love

With her quick wit and good looks, Susan Gilbert charmed Emily Dickinson as perhaps no one else did. Some Dickinson biographers, including Judith Farr, suggest that the poet fell in love with the woman who became her sister-in-law in 1856. In 1858 Emily wrote this poem, included in The Poems of Emily Dickinson, *to the beloved friend who lived beyond the hedge that separated their homes.*

One Sister have I in our house,
And one, a hedge away.
There's only one recorded,
But both belong to me.

One came the road that I came—
And wore my last year's gown—
The other, as a bird her nest,
Builded our hearts among.

She did not sing as we did—
It was a different tune—
Herself to her a music
As Bumblebee of June.

Today is far from Childhood—
But up and down the hills
I held her hand the tighter—
Which shortened all the miles—

And still her hum
The years among,
Deceives the Butterfly;
Still in her Eye
The Violets lie
Mouldered this many May.

I spilt the dew—
But took the morn—
I chose this single star
From out the wide night's numbers—
Sue—forevermore!

one of America's finest poems thanked her sister-in-law for her partial praise of it. She then disclosed her ambitions in a characteristically humble way:

Your praise is good—to me—because I *know* it *knows*—and *suppose*—it *means*—

Could I make you and Austin—proud—sometime—a great way off—'twould give me taller feet—[82]

Dickinson knew she could always count on Sue to read her work, but she began to realize that her sister-in-law would never replace Ben Newton as a critic. Not yet convinced of her own greatness, Dickinson still longed for a mentor—someone who could provide her with the guidance she felt she needed. Reverend Wadsworth "was not content" with the role. Samuel Bowles, the editor of the Springfield *Daily Republican*, had published two of her poems, but he was immersed in the Civil War, which had just broken out. Other than Sue, none of her friends responded to her poems in a way that made Emily think they could assist her. Finally, in 1862 Dickinson came into contact with someone who seemed capable of helping her. He came to her notice not as a schoolmate, nor as a visitor to her home, nor as a preacher. Rather, he spoke to her from the pages of a magazine.

5 Preceptor

Thomas Wentworth Higginson was an ordained Unitarian minister, an author, and a frequent contributor to *The Atlantic Monthly.* By April 1862 no fewer than twenty-two of his essays had appeared in the Boston magazine. Emily Dickinson later revealed that she had read them all. Higginson was the person Dickinson turned to for guidance in 1862.

Like Emily's father, Higginson was active in many social causes. His views differed from those of Edward Dickinson in almost every way, however. Higginson supported women's rights, for example. Edward Dickinson opposed them as a member of the Massachusetts legislature. In 1859 Higginson wrote an article about women's rights that Emily surely saw in *The Atlantic Monthly.* Higginson ridiculed the common attitude toward women's rights with the words: "'John is a fool; Jane is a genius; nevertheless John, being a man, shall learn, lead, make laws, make money; Jane, being woman, shall be ignorant, dependent, disenfranchised, underpaid.'" He added, "This formula really lies at the bottom of the reasoning one hears every day."

Higginson used one of Dickinson's favorite poets, Elizabeth Barrett Browning, as an example of someone who had broken through the limits usually set on women. "Who believed that a poetess could ever be more than an Annot Lyle of the harp, to soothe with sweet melodies the leisure of her lord, until in Elizabeth Barrett's hands the thing became a trumpet," [83] he wrote.

In April 1862 *The Atlantic Monthly* carried a new article by Higginson entitled "Letter to a Young Contributor." Higginson encouraged unpublished writers by stating that "the supposed editorial preju-

Thomas Wentworth Higginson and his daughter aboard a two-seated tricycle. Emily Dickinson wrote to Higginson for literary guidance in 1862.

dice against new or obscure writers" was a myth. On the contrary, he wrote, "to take the lead in bringing forward a new genius is [a] . . . privilege." He urged new writers to avoid stilted, bookish language. "Charge your style with life," he wrote. He also cautioned them against being obscure: "Fight to render your statement clear and attractive, as if your life depended on it: your literary life does depend on it, and, if you fail, relapses into a dead language."

Higginson gave practical tips about preparing the manuscript as well. "Prepare your page so neatly that it shall allure instead of repelling," he advised. "Use good pens, black ink, nice white paper and plenty of it." He believed that a writer, especially a new writer, should not burden an editor with the task of polishing a piece of writing. "On the same principle," Higginson continued, "send your composition in such a shape that it shall not need the slightest literary revision before printing."[84]

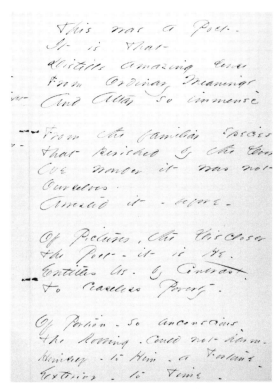

The manuscript of the 1862 poem "This was a Poet—It is That." By the time she wrote these lines, Dickinson had composed approximately 400 poems.

A Fateful Decision

Emily Dickinson saw Higginson's article and decided to write its author. She copied out four of her poems, including three of her most famous works, "Safe in their Alabaster Chambers," "I'll tell you how the Sun rose," and "The nearest Dream recedes—unrealized." She enclosed them with a short letter asking Higginson his opinion of her work.

Mr. Higginson,

Are you too deeply occupied to say if my Verse is alive?

The Mind is so near itself—it cannot see, distinctly—and I have none to ask—

Should you think it breathed—and had you the leisure to tell me, I should feel quick gratitude—

If I make the mistake—that you dared to tell me—would give me sincerer honor—toward you—

I enclose my name—asking you, if you please—Sir—to tell me what is true?

That you will not betray me—it is needless to ask—since Honor is [its] own pawn—[85]

Higginson was intrigued, but puzzled. He could see that the writer from Amherst had "charged her style with life," but she seemed to have ignored his advice about polishing the work to a point where it did

"Tell Me My Fault"

In letter 259 of The Letters of Emily Dickinson, *the poet tells Thomas Wentworth Higginson what kind of criticism she expected to receive from him.*

"Will you tell me my fault, frankly as to yourself, for I had rather wince, than die. Men do not call the surgeon, to commend—the Bone, but to set it, Sir, and fracture within, is more critical. And for this, Preceptor, I shall bring you—Obedience—the Blossom from my Garden, and every gratitude I know. Perhaps you smile at me. I could not stop for that— My Business is Circumference— An ignorance, not of Customs, but if caught with the Dawn—or the Sunset see me—Myself the only Kangaroo among the Beauty, Sir, if you please, it afflicts me, and I thought that instruction would take it away.

Because you have much business, beside the growth of me—you will appoint, yourself, how often I shall come—without your inconvenience. And if at any time— you regret you received me, or I prove a different fabric to that you supposed—you must banish me. . . .

To thank you, baffles me. Are you perfectly powerful? Had I a pleasure you had not, I could delight to bring it.

Your Scholar"

not need "the slightest literary revision." Her poems were filled with oddities— strange capitalization, a peculiar use of dashes, unusual rhymes and rhythms. Higginson might have been able to accept any one of these mannerisms, but he could not embrace them all. At the same time, he sensed that to change any of these elements would change the poem. Many years later, Higginson wrote, "The impression of a wholly new and original poetic genius was as distinct on my mind at the first reading of these four poems as it is now, after thirty years of further knowledge; and with it came the problem never yet solved, what place ought to be assigned in literature to what is so remarkable, yet so elusive of criticism."[86]

Dialogue

Higginson's response to Dickinson's first letter has not survived, but he must have criticized some elements of the poems she enclosed. It appears that he did so gently, though, because Dickinson wrote back, "Thank you for the surgery—it was not so painful as I supposed." She added, "I bring you others—as you ask—though they might not differ."[87] Dickinson enclosed three poems with the letter: "South Winds jostle them," "There came a Day at Summer's full," and "Of all the Sounds despatched abroad."

To better judge Dickinson's work, Higginson inquired about her age, her education, her companions, and her reading. He specifically asked if she was familiar with the poetry of Walt Whitman. One can hardly imagine a poet more different from Dickinson than Whitman, who usually wrote long poems that did not rhyme. Perhaps Higginson was testing to see if Dickinson's free and flexible meter had been influenced by Whitman's free verse style.

Dickinson answered each of Higginson's questions, but she replied to some strangely. She even misled him about some things. For example, Dickinson replied to the question about her age by telling Higginson how long she had been writing. What she wrote, however, was not true. "You asked how old I was? I made no verse—but one or two—until this winter." Actually, Dickinson had composed at least three hundred poems by then. Dickinson was not exactly honest about her schooling, either. "I went to school—but in your manner of phrase—had no education." [88]

Dickinson may have misled Higginson about her age, experience, and education because she was afraid of being rejected by the famous author. She probably reasoned that Higginson would judge her more kindly if he thought she was a beginner. She also may have been playing a kind of game with Higginson, testing to see if he could see through her disguise as a novice. Many years later, Mabel Loomis Todd, a friend of the family, supported this view. She recalled that Emily's brother, Austin Dickinson, "smiled" at Higginson's suggestion that Emily's letters to him were of an "innocent and confiding" nature. "[Austin] says Emily definitely posed in those letters," [89] Todd wrote.

While Dickinson dodged some of Higginson's questions, she answered others directly. "You inquire my Books—For Poets— I have Keats—and Mr and Mrs Browning. For Prose—Mr Ruskin—Sir Thomas Browne—and the Revelations," Dickinson wrote. "You speak of Mr Whitman—I never read his Book," she added. The response Dickinson gave about her companions reads like something out of one of her poems. "You ask of my Companions," she wrote. "Hills—Sir—and the Sundown—and a Dog—large as myself, that my Father bought me— They are better than Beings—because they know—but do not tell." [90]

Emily Dickinson's watch. The poet once confided to T. W. Higginson that she did not learn to tell time until she was fifteen years old, but had been afraid to admit it.

In the letter to Higginson, Dickinson went on to describe her family. "I have a Brother and a Sister—My Mother does not care for thought—and Father, too busy with his Briefs—to notice what we do." By the time Dickinson wrote this letter, the rift between her family's religious beliefs and her own was complete. "They are religious—except me," she wrote, "and address an Eclipse, every morning—whom they call their 'Father.'"[91]

Higginson may have asked about Dickinson's professional ambitions. Had she published her work? Did she hope to? In reply, she described a conversation she had, probably with Samuel Bowles, editor of the Springfield *Daily Republican*, and Josiah Gilbert Holland, who had founded *Scribner's Monthly*.

Two Editors of Journals came to my Father's House, this winter—and asked me for my Mind—and when I asked them "Why," they said I was penurious [stingy]—and they, would use it for the World—[92]

Higginson seems to have liked the poems Dickinson enclosed with her second letter more than the ones she sent with her first. In her next letter, written on June 7, 1862, Dickinson thanked Higginson for his praise of her work. Phrasing her response in her typically metaphorical language, Dickinson stated that Higginson's kind words reminded her of support she had received before, no doubt from Ben Newton. "Your letter gave no Drunkenness, because I tasted Rum before . . . yet I

"Are You Too Deeply Occupied to Say If My Verse Is Alive?"

Emily Dickinson enclosed four poems along with her first letter to Thomas Wentworth Higginson. This work, included in The Poems of Emily Dickinson, *is one of them.*

I'll tell you how the Sun rose—
A Ribbon at a time—
The Steeples swam in Amethyst—
The news, like Squirrels, ran—
The Hills untied their Bonnets—
The Bobolinks—begun—
Then I said softly to myself—
"That must have been the Sun"!
But how he set—I know not—
There seemed a purple stile
That little Yellow boys and girls
Were climbing all the while—
Till when they reached the other side,
A Dominie in Gray—
Put gently up the evening Bars—
And led the flock away—

have had few pleasures so deep as your opinion, and if I tried to thank you, my tears would block my tongue."[93]

Caught off Guard

Because Higginson had criticized Dickinson's work in his first letter, his praise in the second letter appears to have caught the poet off guard. "Your second letter surprised me, and for a moment, swung— I had not supposed it." If Dickinson meant for "swung" to refer to herself, and not to the letter, it appears that the poet staggered, perhaps almost fainted, upon reading Higginson's praise. She admitted that the criticism of the first letter might have been deserved. "Your first—gave no dishonor, because the True—are not ashamed." She confided, however, that Higginson's criticism had stuck with her and dampened the fire of her creativity. "I thanked you for your justice—but could not drop the Bells whose jingling cooled my Tramp." For Dickinson, the criticism in the first letter made the praise in the second more meaningful. "Perhaps the Balm, seemed better, because you bled me, first,"[94] Dickinson concluded.

Perhaps responding to Dickinson's account of the two editors who had asked for her "Mind," Higginson advised the Amherst poet not to publish her work, at least for a while. Dickinson's reply is one of the most famous, and most scrutinized, things she ever wrote. Despite the fact that three of her poems had already appeared in print, Dickinson claimed to have no interest in publishing her work.

I smile when you suggest that I delay "to publish"—that being foreign to my thought, as Firmament to Fin—

If fame belonged to me, I could not escape her—if she did not, the longest day would pass me on the chase—and the approbation of my Dog, would forsake me—then— My Barefoot-Rank is better—[95]

Some Dickinson scholars have taken this passage at face value. They believe the Amherst poet had no interest in publication or fame. They argue that Dickinson valued her privacy too much to embark on a career that might bring her into contact with more people. Other scholars disagree. They think Dickinson was covering up her disappointment at Higginson's lukewarm response to her work. After all, she had written to Higginson after reading his article about how to get published. Had Higginson urged her to publish, these scholars reason, Dickinson probably would have done so. Since he did not, Dickinson pretended to have no interest in publishing.

A New Stage

Regardless of whether Dickinson had decided against publication before she wrote to Higginson or only lost interest in it after his tepid reception to her work, the letter she wrote in June 1862 marked a new stage in her career. From that point forward, Dickinson would write only for herself, her friends, and perhaps posterity. She would not pursue what she later called "the Auction / Of the Mind of Man."[96]

The June 1862 letter also marks the first time that Dickinson responded to Higginson's criticism of her work. Apparently

Higginson disapproved of Dickinson's meter. The thirty-one-year-old poet did not defend her work. "You think my gait 'spasmodic'— I am in danger—Sir," she wrote. "You think me 'uncontrolled'— I have no Tribunal." [97]

Some scholars believe that Dickinson was weighing the possibility that her meter was flawed. To support this view, they point to a letter she wrote two months later. She enclosed two more poems and began her note, "Are these more orderly? I thank you for the Truth." [98]

Other scholars dispute the notion that Dickinson saw anything wrong with her style. These scholars believe that Dickinson was playing yet another game with Higginson. They argue that she merely pretended to be a student, all the while knowing that she was far more advanced in her thinking than her so-called teacher would ever be. As proof of their position, these scholars point to the fact that Dickinson never adopted the changes that Higginson suggested.

Preceptor and Friend

Dickinson may or may not have respected Higginson's criticism, but she surely valued his friendship. "Would you have time to be the 'friend' you should think I need?" Dickinson asked Higginson in the June 1862 letter. She promised not to demand too much of the busy writer. "I have a little shape—it would not crowd your Desk—nor make much Racket as the Mouse, that dents your Galleries," she continued. With Ben Newton gone, Reverend Wadsworth uninterested, and Susan Gilbert busy with her own family, Dickinson longed for someone with whom to share her work, her thoughts, her life. She phrased her request as clearly as possible. "If I might bring you what I do—not so frequent to trouble you—and ask you if I told it clear—'twould be control, to me," she wrote. "Will you be my Preceptor, Mr Higginson?" [99]

Whatever his shortcomings, Thomas Wentworth Higginson sensed something extraordinary about the young woman who had written to him from Amherst. He could have ignored her or politely brushed her off. To his credit, however, he did not. Instead, he accepted the role of being Dickinson's preceptor, or teacher, reading her poems and offering his judgments when possible.

Thomas Wentworth Higginson. A well-known author in his own time, Higginson achieved literary immortality through his friendship with Emily Dickinson.

Dickinson Describes Herself

In the summer of 1862, Thomas Wentworth Higginson asked Emily Dickinson to send him a photograph of herself. In its place, Dickinson included the following description of herself in letter number 259 of The Letters of Emily Dickinson.

"July 1862

To T. W. Higginson

Could you believe me—without? I had no portrait, now, but am small, like the Wren, and my Hair is bold, like the Chestnut Bur—and my eyes, like the Sherry in the Glass, that the Guest leaves— Would this do just as well?

It often alarms Father— He says Death might occur, and he has Molds of all the rest—but has no Mold of me, but I noticed the Quick wore off those things, in a few days, and forestall the dishonor— You will think no caprice of me—"

More importantly, Higginson became Dickinson's friend. At the time she wrote to Higginson, Dickinson was in the throes of some sort of mental crisis. "I had a terror—since September—I could tell to none," she confided in her second letter to Higginson. In her third letter, she described the "palsy" she felt when beholding "a sudden light on Orchards, or a new fashion in the wind." [100]

Vivid as these descriptions are, they provide only a hint of the inner turmoil that raged within the poet. During this time, Dickinson was writing poems at the rate of one per day, according to Thomas Johnson's count. Many of these works depict a mind at war with itself. "I felt a Funeral, in my Brain"; "After great pain, a formal feeling comes"; "It was not Death, for I stood up"; "The Soul has Bandaged moments"; "The Brain, within its Groove"; "The Battle fought between the Soul"—these are just a few of the poems Dickinson composed during this difficult time. [101]

Higginson's letters to Dickinson have not survived, but his friendship touched her deeply. "The 'hand you stretch me in the Dark,' I put mine in," she wrote to him toward the end of the June 1862 letter. Seven years later, Dickinson reflected on the bond she had formed with Higginson in the feverish summer of 1862. "Of our greatest acts we are ignorant," she wrote to Higginson in 1869. "You were not aware that you saved my Life." [102]

There is no reason to doubt that she was telling the truth.

6 The Soul Selects Her Own Society

Always a private person, Emily Dickinson began to withdraw from face-to-face contact with other people at about the same time that she began her correspondence with Thomas Wentworth Higginson. By 1862 Dickinson had stopped venturing out of her house. She even shrank from meetings with longtime friends.

In November 1862 she refused to see Samuel Bowles when he paid a visit. Afterward, Bowles sent Dickinson a bat, a piece from the game of shuttlecock. The memento was designed to remind her of their friendship. In a letter to Bowles, Dickinson apologized for her behavior, suggesting that she withdrew so that Lavinia and Austin could have the visitor to themselves.

> I did not need the little bat—to enforce your memory—for that can stand alone, like the best Brocade. . . . Because I did not see you, Vinnie and Austin, up-braided me— They did not know I gave my part that they might have the more—but then the Prophet has not fame in his immediate Town—[103]

The episode with Bowles was not an isolated event. Ever since her return from Mount Holyoke Female Seminary, Dickinson had found excuses to avoid contact with other people. By 1869 her withdrawal

from the world had become a habit. "I do not cross my Father's ground to any House or town,"[104] she wrote to Thomas Wentworth Higginson. This was not an exaggeration. For the last twenty years of her life,

Samuel Bowles was the editor of the Springfield Daily Republican *and a close friend of the* Dickinsons.

The Dickinson Homestead on Main Street in Amherst. Originally built by Samuel Fowler Dickinson, the large, brick house was sold by the Dickinsons, then repurchased in 1855. Emily's bedroom windows are in the upper left corner of the house.

the poet never left the Dickinson Homestead. She even sent Lavinia in her place to be fitted for the dresses she wore.

A Sacred Quiet

Dickinson biographers have long debated the reasons for the poet's retreat from the world. Lavinia Dickinson suggested that her sister withdrew from contact to preserve her energies for her art. "She was a very busy person herself. She had to think—she was the only one of us who had that to do,"[105] Lavinia once said. Susan Gilbert Dickinson agreed that Dickinson's retreat was a matter of choice on the part of the poet. After her sister-in-law died, Sue reflected on "the facts of her seclusion and intellectual brilliancy":

> As she passed on in life, her sensitive nature shrank from much personal contact with the world, and more and more turned to her own large wealth of individual resources for companionship, sitting thenceforth, as some one said of her, "in the light of her own fire." Not

disappointed with the world, not an invalid until within the past two years, not from any lack of sympathy, not because she was insufficient for any mental work or social career—her endowments being so exceptional—but the "mesh of her soul," as Browning calls the body, was too rare, and the sacred quiet of her own home proved the fit atmosphere for her worth and work.[106]

Some of Dickinson's biographers have disagreed with the notion that the poet's withdrawal from the world was the result of a conscious choice. They suggest that some kind of mental disorder—such as agoraphobia, the fear of crowds—turned Dickinson into a recluse.

A Curious Habit

At about the same time that Dickinson began to withdraw from the world, she also began to dress only in white. The reasons for this unusual practice, too, have been debated by scholars. Thomas Johnson and others have suggested that the poet's decision to dress in white was linked to her feelings for Charles Wadsworth. According to this theory, Dickinson fell in love with Wadsworth when she met him in Philadelphia. At that point, the young poet began to see herself as a kind of secret bride of the already married minister.

For support of this notion, these scholars point to Dickinson's poems about being a bride. "A solemn thing—it was—I said / A woman—white—to be," begins a poem Dickinson wrote in 1861, the year Charles Wadsworth moved from Philadelphia to San Francisco. "The World—stands—solemner—to me— / Since I was wed—to Him" begins an 1862 poem. "Mine—by the Right of the White Election! / Mine—by the Royal Seal!" starts another poem written in 1862. "What right have I—to be a Bride—," Dickinson asked in a third 1862 work.[107] In this poem, she describes how she will no longer wear dun (dark) dresses since she is now "a Bride."

Me to adorn—How—tell—
Trinket—to make Me beautiful—
Fabrics of Cashmere—
Never a Gown of Dun—more—
Raiment instead—of Pompadour—
For Me—My soul—to wear . . .

Fashion My Spirit quaint—white—
Quick—like a Liquor—
Gay—like Light—
Bring Me my best Pride—
No more ashamed—
No more to hide—
Meek—let it be—too proud—for Pride—
Baptized—this Day—A Bride—[108]

Judith Farr agrees that these poems are linked to Dickinson's decision to wear white, but she disputes the idea that the secret "marriage" was to Charles Wadsworth or any other man Dickinson knew.

If "Wedded" means married to a man, however, it is useful to point out that

Why Did Dickinson Retreat from the World?

In The Passion of Emily Dickinson, *Judith Farr described the competing theories of why the poet retreated from the world.*

"Since Martha Dickinson Bianchi's espousal of her mother's account in *The Life and Letters of Emily Dickinson,* her aunt's readers have been offered many other explanations for the poet's semiretirement. They have been asked to consider the hermetic Dickinson as an agoraphobe; as reclusive to please her father; as a sufferer from separation anxiety or from the need to create a private religion in retreat; as a lesbian in love with a widowed friend of Sue's and guiltily hiding from that self-discovery; as a plagiarist afraid to be found out; as an anorexic for whom renunciation was better than food; as the damaged victim of a love affair, which included abortion."

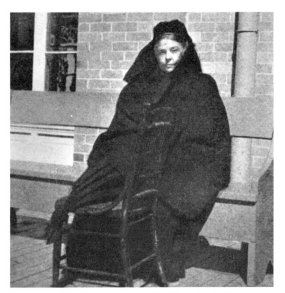

Susan Gilbert Dickinson in 1897. After Dickinson's death, Sue described her sister-in-law's retreat from the world as a conscious choice.

Dickinson's poem was probably written in 1861—brides did not customarily wear white in the United States until the late 1870s. It took almost forty years for Queen Victoria's white satin, lace, and orange blossoms, copied in England after 1840, to appear in American weddings.[109]

Farr notes that women preparing to be Catholic nuns "almost always wore white." For this reason, Farr argues, "There is every reason to suppose that Emily Dickinson had in mind . . . the nun's vocation as a bride of her master, Christ." Given that Dickinson was not Catholic, nor even a confessed Christian, Farr quickly adds that Dickinson's supposed decision to become a nun was not literal. Rather, Farr concludes, "that vocation is taken as itself a metaphor of the artist's calling."[110]

In their book *The Madwoman in the Attic*, Sandra M. Gilbert and Susan Gubar suggest that Dickinson's decision to wear white did not reflect a deep commitment to anyone. Rather, they argue, Dickinson was engaged in an elaborate form of role-playing. By dressing in white, Gilbert and Gubar maintain, Dickinson was "impersonating simultaneously a 'little maid' in white, a fierce virgin in white, a nun in white, a bride in white, a madwoman in white, a dead woman in white, and a ghost."[111] Cynthia Griffin Wolff has a much simpler explanation. She writes that Dickinson started wearing white because it was "one of her favorite colors (perhaps because it is flattering to her fair complexion and vivid chestnut-red hair)."[112]

One of the dresses owned by Emily Dickinson. Around 1862, the Amherst poet began to dress only in white.

Memorable Quotes

After paying his first visit to Emily Dickinson, Thomas Wentworth Higginson jotted down some of the memorable things she said. In letter 342a of The Letters of Emily Dickinson, *Higginson sent an account of the poet's comments to his wife.*

"'Truth is such a *rare* thing it is delightful to tell it.'

'I find ecstasy in living—the mere sense of living is joy enough.'

'Women talk: men are silent: that is why I dread women.'

'How do most people live without any thoughts. There are many people in the world (you must have noticed them in the street) How do they live. How do they get the strength to put on their clothes in the morning.'

'When I lost the use of my Eyes it was a comfort to think there were so few real *books* that I could easily find someone to read me all of them.'

I asked if she never felt want of employment, never going off the place & never seeing any visitor. 'I never thought of conceiving that I could ever have the slightest approach to such a want in all future time' (& added) 'I feel that I have not expressed myself strongly enough.'

'I never knew how to tell time by the clock till I was 15. My father thought he had taught but I did not understand & I was afraid to say I did not & afraid to ask any one else lest he should know.'

They were then little things in short dresses with their feet on the rungs of the chair. After the first book she thought in ecstasy 'This then is a book! And there are more of them!'

After long disuse of her eyes she read Shakespeare & thought why is any other book needed.

When I said I would come again *some time* she said 'Say in a long time, that will be nearer. Some time is nothing.'"

However, it is hard to imagine that a woman who kept no picture of herself and avoided face-to-face contact even with longtime friends began to dress in white simply because it looked good on her. Clearly, wearing white symbolized some sort of commitment to Dickinson. The fact that she began to wear white at the same time she began to retreat from society suggests that the two actions were linked. Starting in 1862, Dickinson decided to reserve herself for a higher purpose—

romantic, artistic, religious, or all three. That year she wrote:

> The Soul selects her own Society—
> Then—shuts the Door—
> To her divine Majority—
> Present no more—
> Unmoved—she notes the Chariots—
>   pausing—
> At her low Gate—
> Unmoved—an Emperor be kneeling
> Upon her Mat—
> I've known her—from an ample
>   nation—
> Choose One—
> Then—close the Valves of her
>   attention—
> Like Stone—[113]

After 1862 the pace at which Dickinson composed her poems slowed somewhat, but the poet remained highly productive. In 1863 she wrote 140 poems; in 1864 she wrote 172; in 1865 she wrote 84. From 1866 through 1886, she wrote another 708 poems, an average of about 35 per year. She also wrote more than 700 letters during those years.

Defeated

Dickinson did not pursue fame during these years, but she found it increasingly difficult to escape it. In 1866, for example, Susan Gilbert Dickinson passed Emily Dickinson's poem "A narrow Fellow in the Grass," to Samuel Bowles at the Springfield *Daily Republican*. During the week of February 17, the poem appeared in both the daily and weekly editions of the paper under the title "The Snake."

Emily Dickinson was upset—for two reasons. First, she feared that Thomas Wentworth Higginson would see the poem and think that she had deceived him about her desire not to publish. Second, the poem had been altered without her permission. She immediately wrote to Higginson to apprise him of the situation.

> Lest you meet my Snake and suppose I deceive it was robbed of me—defeated too the third line by the punctuation. The third and fourth were one— I had told you I did not print— I feared you might think me ostensible.[114]

Emily Dickinson's bedroom in the Homestead. Dickinson composed most of her 1,775 poems in this room, often working while the rest of her family slept.

In the same letter, Dickinson answered Higginson's request to meet her. As was her custom, Dickinson provided an excuse for her inability to travel beyond the grounds of the family mansion. "I am uncertain of Boston," she wrote. "I had promised to visit my Physician for a few days in May, but Father objects because he is in the habit of me." Instead, Dickinson suggested that Higginson visit her. "Is it more far to Amherst?"[115] she asked.

A few months later, Higginson again asked Dickinson to visit. Her reply was the same. "I must omit Boston. Father prefers so. He likes me to travel with him but objects that I visit." This time her invitation to Higginson to visit Amherst was more direct. "Might I entrust you, as my Guest to the Amherst Inn?"[116] she asked.

Higginson did not accept. In May 1869 he wrote again to invite Dickinson to Boston. "I have the greatest desire to see you, always feeling that perhaps if I could once take you by the hand I might be something to you; but till then you only enshroud yourself in this fiery mist & I cannot reach you, but only rejoice in the rare sparkles of light. . . . You must come down to Boston sometimes?"[117] Higginson wrote.

A Remarkable Experience

Dickinson replied in June. Once again, she declined to go to Boston but invited Higginson to Amherst. "Could it please your convenience to come so far as Amherst I should be very glad,"[118] she wrote. Higginson realized that if he was ever going to meet the poet from Amherst, he would have to travel to her home. On August 16, 1870, he did so. That night he wrote into his diary, "To Amherst, arrived there at 2 Saw Prest Stearns, Mrs. Banfield & Miss Dickinson (twice) a remarkable experience, quite equalling my expectation." The same evening, he recounted the meeting in a letter to his wife:

A step like a pattering child's in entry & in glided a little plain woman with two smooth bands of reddish hair & a face a little like Belle Dove's; not plainer—with no good feature—in a very plain & exquisitely clean white pique & a blue net worsted shawl. She came to me with two day lilies which she put in a sort of childlike way into my hand & said "These are my introduction" in a soft frightened breathless childlike voice—& added under her breath Forgive me if I am frightened; I never see strangers & hardly know what I say—but she talked soon & thenceforward continuously—& deferentially—sometimes stopping to ask me to talk instead of her—but readily recommencing.[119]

The next day, Higginson again wrote to his wife, adding a few more details about his meeting with Dickinson. "I never was with any one who drained my nerve power so much," he wrote. "Without touching her, she drew from me. I am glad not to live near her."[120] Twenty years later, Higginson recalled the meeting in an article for *The Atlantic Monthly.*

The impression undoubtedly made on me was that of an excess of tension, and of an abnormal life. Perhaps in time I could have got beyond that somewhat overstrained relation which not my will, but her needs, had forced upon us. Certainly I should have been most glad to bring it down to the level of simple truth and every-day com-

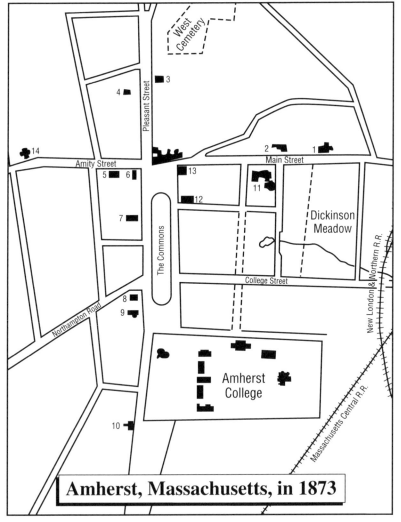

1. Emily Dickinson's birthplace and home, 1830–1840, 1855–1886.
2. William Austin Dickinson's house, built 1856.
3. Emily Dickinson's home, 1840–1855.
4. The Primary School.
5. Amherst Academy, 1814–1861.
6. Boltwood's Tavern, later the Amherst House.
7. The Baptist Church.
8. The Meeting House, later College Hall.
9. Morgan Library (Amherst College).
10. Birthplace of Helen M. Fiske (Helen Hunt Jackson).
11. The Village Church and Parsonage.
12. Grace Church (Episcopal).
13. The Town Hall.
14. William Cutler's house, where Susan Gilbert lived.

radeship; but it was not altogether easy. She was much too enigmatical a being for me to solve in an hour's interview, and an instinct told me that the slightest attempt at cross-examination would make her withdraw into her shell.[121]

While Dickinson's words were fresh in his mind, Higginson jotted down the most striking of them. Among the most important comments Higginson remembered was Dickinson's definition of poetry. "If I read a book [and] it makes my whole body so cold no fire ever can warm me I know *that* is poetry. If I feel physically as if the top of my head were taken off, I know *that* is poetry. These are the only ways I know it. Is there any other way."[122]

Though it lasted only a few hours, Higginson's visit to the Dickinson Homestead cemented the bond that had formed between the author and the poet. Afterward, their friendship became warmer; their letters, more personal. It was a relationship destined to bring fame to them both.

Chapter

7 Distant Strains of Triumph

Dickinson's life continued in more or less the same fashion that Higginson found it until June 16, 1874. On that day, Dickinson's father died. "Father does not live with us now—he lives in a new house," Dickinson wrote to her cousins Louise and Frances Norcross. "Though it was built in an hour it is better than this."[123] Austin Dickinson's reaction to his father's death speaks volumes about the emotional distance Squire Dickinson maintained with his children. When Edward Dickinson's body arrived from Boston, where he had died, Austin impulsively kissed his dead father's forehead. "There, father, I never dared do that while you were living,"[124] said Austin.

One year after Emily Dickinson's father died, her mother was paralyzed with a stroke. For the next seven years, Dickinson cared for her mother. The stroke was the last in a long series of illnesses endured by Emily Norcross Dickinson. Many of these illnesses are clearly documented. For example, Edward Dickinson added a note to one of Emily's letters to Austin describing an abscessed tooth Mrs. Dickinson had: "Mother has been severely afflicted with the Neuralgia arising from her front tooth . . . it was lanced . . . & she is now relieved."[125] Other bouts of sickness are more mysterious, however. "Mother has been an invalid since we came *home*," Emily wrote in 1867. "I don't know what her sickness is."[126]

In his book *After Great Pain*, Dr. John Cody argues that Emily's mother was a life-

William Austin Dickinson, Emily's older brother, is pictured here circa 1890.

Dickinson's Last Afternoon with Her Father

A month after her father died, Emily Dickinson wrote to Thomas Wentworth Higginson. In letter number 418 of The Letters of Emily Dickinson, *the poet describes the last afternoon she spent with her father.*

"The last Afternoon that my Father lived, though with no premonition—I preferred to be with him, and invented an absence for Mother, Vinnie being asleep. He seemed peculiarly pleased as I oftenest stayed with myself, and remarked as the Afternoon withdrew, he 'would like it not to end.'

His pleasure almost embarrassed me and my Brother coming—I suggested they walk. Next morning I woke him for the train—and saw him no more.

His Heart was pure and terrible and I think no other like it exists."

Edward Dickinson, Emily's father.

long hypochondriac who transferred her fear of illness and death to her daughter. According to Cody, Emily Dickinson wrote hundreds of poems about death in large part because she grew up in a household gripped by neurotic, or excessive, fears.

Richard B. Sewall, author of *The Life of Emily Dickinson*, disagrees with Cody's conclusion. "Nothing in the Dickinson annals suggests Mrs. Dickinson as the source of such anxieties in any of her children," Sewall writes. In Sewall's opinion, Dickinson returned to the theme of death hundreds of times in her poems and letters not out of a compulsion, but because it fascinated her as a writer. "What occupied her as a mature artist and thinker was death as an existential phenomenon and as the central religious mystery, to be probed and pondered with the objectivity, almost, of the clinician and the philosopher." [127]

A Reversal of Roles

Sewall based his conclusion, in part, on the manner in which Emily and Lavinia cared for their stricken mother. "It is worth noting that we have no bitter complaints from either daughter—a hint of fatigue now and then, and preoccupation, but no resentment," [128] writes Sewall. If anything, the role of nurse brought out Emily's tender side.

> The responsibility of Pathos is almost more than the responsibility of Care. Mother will never walk. She still makes her little Voyages from her Bed to her Chair in a Strong Man's Arms—probably that will be all. . . . To read to her—to fan her—to tell her "Health would come Tomorrow," and make the Counterfeit look real—to explain *why* "the Grasshopper is a Burden"—because it is not as new a Grasshopper as it was—this is so ensuing, that I hardly have said "Good Morning, Mother," when I hear myself saying, "Mother,—Good Night—"[129]

Throughout her life, Dickinson had been closer to her father than her mother. She found that the time she spent caring for her mother had strengthened the bond between them. "We were never intimate Mother and Children while she was our mother," Dickinson wrote to Mrs. J. G. Holland, "but Mines in the same Ground meet by tunneling, and when she became our Child, the Affection came. . . ."[130]

When her mother died on November 14, 1882, Emily wrote to Mrs. Holland, "The dear Mother that could not walk, has *flown*. It never occurred to us that though she had not Limbs, she had *Wings*—and she soared from us unexpectedly as a summoned Bird."[131]

Praise from Afar

During her mother's long illness, Emily Dickinson received a letter from the famous novelist and poet Helen Hunt Jack-

Helen Hunt Jackson was a famous novelist and poet. She instantly recognized the greatness in Emily Dickinson's work.

son. Jackson, who had grown up in Amherst and gone to school with Dickinson, found out about her old schoolmate's literary endeavors from Thomas Wentworth Higginson. Unlike Higginson, Jackson had no doubts about the quality of Dickinson's work. "I have a little manuscript volume with a few of your verses in it—and I read them very often," Jackson wrote to Dickinson in 1875. "You are a great poet—and it is wrong to the day you live in, that you will not sing aloud."[132]

Despite Jackson's urgings, Dickinson refused to publish. In 1876, however, Jackson hatched a plan to finally bring Dickinson's work the attention she believed it deserved. In August, she asked Dickinson if she could submit one of her poems to an anthology of poetry to be published by Roberts Brothers. The book was to be part of the highly popular publishing project known as the "no name" series. Roberts Brothers had published a series of books anonymously, allowing readers and critics to guess who wrote them. Jackson thought the proposed poetry volume would be the perfect forum for Dickinson.

> I enclose to you a circular which may interest you. When the volume of Verse is published in this series, I shall contribute to it: and I want to persuade you to. Surely in the shelter of such *double* anonymousness as that will be, you need not shrink. I want to see some of your verses in print. Unless you forbid me, I will send some that I have. May I?[133]

Dickinson apparently did not respond to the request. A few months later, Jackson visited Dickinson at her home and renewed the request. Dickinson gave an account of this meeting to Thomas Wentworth Higginson and enclosed the circular describing the publishing project. She also asked his advice about publishing her work.

> Dear friend—
> Are you willing to tell me what is right? Mrs Jackson—of Colorado—was with me a few moments this week, and wished me to write for this— I told her I was unwilling, and she asked me why?— I said I was incapable and she seemed not to believe me and asked me not to decide for a few Days— meantime, she would write me— She was so sweetly noble, I would regret to estrange her, and if you would be willing to give me a note saying you disap-

prove it, and thought me unfit, she would believe you— I am sorry to flee so often to my safest friend, but hope he permits me—[134]

Since the circular described only the fiction books, Higginson apparently thought that Jackson had asked Dickinson to write a story. "It is always hard to judge for another of the bent of inclination or range of talent," he wrote to Dickinson, "but I should not have thought of advising you to write stories, as it would not seem to me to be in your line."[135] Dickinson immediately wrote back to clear things up. "It was not stories she asked of me," Dickinson explained about Jackson's request. "But may I tell her just the same that you don't prefer it? Thank you, if I may, for it almost seems sordid to refuse from myself again."[136]

Helen Hunt Jackson had not achieved renown by being easily discouraged, however. As the deadline for submissions to the book approached, she once again raised the subject in a letter to Dickinson.

> Would it be of any use to ask you once more for one or two of your poems, to come out in the volume of "no name" poetry which is to be published before long by Roberts Bros.? If you will give me permission I will copy them— sending them in my own handwriting—and promise never to tell any one, not even the publishers, whose the poems are. Could you not bear this much publicity? Only you and I would recognize the poems. I wish very much that you would do this— and I think you would have much amusement in seeing to whom the critics, those shrewd guessers, would ascribe your verses.[137]

To Jackson's dismay, Dickinson still refused. Underestimating Dickinson's resolve, perhaps, Jackson may have already passed one of Dickinson's poems along to the publisher without the poet's consent. She arranged to call on Dickinson in October to renew her plea for a poem. The day after the meeting, Jackson wrote again to Dickinson, asking permission to send Roberts Brothers one of her favorite of Dickinson's poems, "Success is counted sweetest."

> Now—will you send me the poem? No—will you let me send the "Success"—which I know by heart—to Roberts Bros for the Masque of Poets? If you will, it will give me great pleasure. I ask it as a personal favor to myself— Can you refuse the only thing I perhaps shall ever ask at your hands?[138]

Dickinson at last gave in. In December 1878 Roberts Brothers published the volume of anonymous verse. "Success is counted sweetest" appeared beside the work of many then-famous poets, including John Greenleaf Whittier, Louisa May Alcott, Helen Hunt Jackson, and Dickinson's own favorite, Ralph Waldo Emerson. In what must have been a gratifying turn of events, many critics guessed that Emerson was the author of Dickinson's poem. "If anything in the volume was contributed by Emerson, we should consider these lines upon 'Success' most probably his,"[139] wrote a reviewer for *Literary World*. The magazine then reprinted the entire poem for its readers to judge for themselves.

The publication of "Success" opened doors for Dickinson, but she chose not to pass through them. Thomas Niles, the editor of *A Masque of Poets*, sent Dickinson an encouraging note along with a copy of the book. Dickinson began to correspond with

---

Success

In 1878 Helen Hunt Jackson persuaded Emily Dickinson to allow one of her poems to appear in a book of anonymous verse entitled A Masque of Poets. *The editor of the book, Thomas Niles, changed the wording and punctuation of the poem. The poet's original version was published in* The Complete Poems of Emily Dickinson.

Success is counted sweetest
By those who ne'er succeed.
To comprehend a nectar
Requires sorest need.

Not one of all the purple Host
Who took the Flag today
Can tell the definition
So clear of Victory

As he defeated—dying—
On whose forbidden ear
The distant strains of triumph
Burst agonized and clear!

The famous essayist and poet Ralph Waldo Emerson. Some critics guessed that he had written Dickinson's poem "Success."

How happy is the little Stone
That rambles on the Road alone,
And does'nt care about Careers
And Exigencies never fears—
Whose Coat of elemental Brown
A passing Universe put on,
And independent as the Sun
Associates or glows alone,
Fulfilling absolute Decree
In casual simplicity—[142]

Dickinson was far too artful of a writer to have placed this poem in an envelope addressed to Thomas Niles without a reason. Clearly, the poet identified herself with the "little Stone," and the poem was meant as a reply to Niles's suggestion that she publish more of her work. Like the stone, Dickinson implies, she is "happy" to go about her business "alone," free of "fears" and cares of the world. She does not need "careers" to fulfill her destiny, a fate which was set by "absolute Decree." Instead, "independent as the Sun," she will continue to "glow alone."

An Offer Ignored

A few months after this exchange, Niles sent Dickinson a book she had inquired about, a biography of the author Marian Evans, whose pen name was George Eliot. In March 1883, as a token of her gratitude for this gift, Dickinson sent Niles a note with two more poems. She then sent the editor her copy of the poems of Emily and Charlotte Brontë. Niles returned Dickinson's book with a note containing an unmistakable request to publish her work.

Niles, and in 1882 Niles broached the subject of publishing a book of her poems.

> "H. H." [Helen Hunt Jackson] once told me that she wished you could be induced to publish a volume of poems. I should not want to say how highly she praised them, but to such an extent that I wish also that you could.[140]

Dickinson replied with her usual modesty, "The kind but incredible opinion of 'H.H.' and yourself I would like to deserve— Would you accept a Pebble I think I gave to her, though I am not sure."[141] The pebble Dickinson referred to was a poem she enclosed, "How happy is the little Stone," a work that seems to sum up Dickinson's own attitude about "careers."

> If I may presume to say so, I will take instead a M.S. [manuscript] collection

of your poems, that is, if you want to give them to the world through the medium of a publisher.[143]

Apparently, she did not. She failed to forward as much as a single packet of her work to the eager publisher. Probably she had no intention of doing so; or perhaps she did but was distracted by a series of tragic events. During the years of her correspondence with Niles, not only had Dickinson's mother died (1882), but so had Samuel Bowles (1878), Dr. Holland (1881), Reverend Wadsworth (1882), and her cousin Willie Dickinson (1883). In May 1883, just two months after Niles had asked for a manuscript of Dickinson's poems, one of the Dickinsons' closest friends, Judge Otis P. Lord, suffered a stroke. In October 1883 Dickinson experienced an especially painful loss. Her eight-year-old nephew Thomas Gilbert Dickinson contracted typhoid fever and died within three days. Dickinson wrote a brief letter of condolence to Gilbert's mother, Susan Gilbert Dickinson. The letter ended with a poem about Gilbert's journey into an afterlife:

> Pass to thy Rendezvous of Light,
> Pangless except for us—
> Who slowly ford the Mystery
> Which thou hast leaped across![144]

Though she was able to compose these hope-filled lines for Sue, Dickinson was devastated by the loss of her nephew. She stayed in bed or barely functioned for several weeks afterward.

Thomas Gilbert Dickinson, Emily Dickinson's beloved nephew. His death at the age of eight sent Dickinson into a deep depression.

A few months after Dickinson regained her strength, Judge Lord died. That same month, June 1884, Helen Hunt Jackson fell down the stairs of her home and broke her leg. Dickinson wrote to her literary friend, wishing her a speedy recovery. Jackson thanked Dickinson for her note, then resumed her efforts to persuade the poet to publish her work. "What portfolios of verses you must have," Jackson accurately guessed. "It is wrong to your 'day & generation' that you will not give them light. . . . I do not think we have a right to with hold from the world a word or a thought any more than a *deed*, which might help a single soul." [145]

Dickinson wrote back to Jackson, enclosed more poems, but did not follow up on Jackson's suggestion. Perhaps having the esteem of the woman that Emerson had called America's greatest poet gave Dickinson all the satisfaction she needed. The two women continued their correspondence throughout 1884 and the first half of 1885. In August, Jackson died of cancer. Dickinson wrote to Jackson's widower—William S. Jackson—her publisher, and her minister, asking details about her death, which had come as something of a shock to Dickinson. When Higginson wrote to Dickinson during the winter of 1885, asking if she had heard about Jackson's death, Dickinson acknowledged that she had. "I think she would rather have stayed with us, but perhaps she will learn the customs of Heaven," [146] Dickinson mused.

Called Back

By the time Dickinson responded to Higginson's letter, she herself was sick. She was suffering from nephritis, a kidney disease. "I have been very ill, Dear friend, since November," Dickinson wrote to her longtime friend, "bereft of Book and Thought, by the Doctor's reproof, but begin to roam my room now." [147]

At the close of her letter to Higginson, Dickinson recalled the biblical story of how Jacob had wrestled with a stranger, only to find out later that he was an angel. Before he released the angel from his hold, Jacob told the angel that he would not let him go until he had blessed him. Dickinson, who had wrestled with matters of faith her entire adult life, loved the story of the human who had struggled with the heavenly being, bested him, and sent him away with a blessing. "Pugilist and Poet, Jacob was correct," [148] Dickinson ended her letter. It was the last time Higginson would ever hear from the shy poet whose life he had "saved" so many years before.

In May of 1886, Dickinson's condition worsened. She wrote a brief note to her beloved cousins Louise and Frances Norcross. "Little Cousins, Called back—Emily," [149] she wrote. On the thirteenth of May, Dickinson slipped into a coma. At about six in the evening on Saturday, May 15, she died.

If Fame Belonged to Me

Lavinia Dickinson knew that her sister had written a great deal of poetry, but she was shocked when she found more than 1,700 poems in the bottom drawer of Emily Dickinson's bureau. As she looked through the carefully sewn packets of verse, Lavinia decided to do what Emily had long resisted. She would find a publisher for her sister's verse.

Lavinia asked Mabel Loomis Todd, the wife of a professor at Amherst College and a friend of Emily's, to transcribe the poems. Mabel Todd had moved to Amherst in 1881 when she was twenty-four years old. Her husband, David Peck Todd, had been hired to teach astronomy at Amherst College. Through their association with the college, the Todds soon met Austin and Susan Dickinson.

In February 1882 Susan Dickinson shared her sister-in-law's poetry with Mabel Todd. Afterward Todd wrote in her diary, "Went in the afternoon to Mrs. Dickinson's. She read me some strange poems by Emily Dickinson. They are full of power." Eventually, Mabel was invited to the Dickinson Homestead. Though she never saw Emily face-to-face, she did play the piano and sing for her. She wrote a detailed account of an early visit in her journal.

His [Austin's] sister Emily is called in Amherst "the myth." She has not been out of her house for fifteen years. . . . She writes the strangest poems, & very remarkable ones. She is in many respects a genius. She wears always white, & has her hair arranged as was the fashion fifteen years ago when she went into retirement. She wanted me to come & sing to her, but she would not see me. . . . It was odd to think, as my voice rang out through the big silent house that Miss Emily in her weird white dress was outside in the shadow hearing every word, & the mother, bed-ridden for years was listening up stairs. When I stopped Emily sent me in a glass of rich sherry & a poem written as I sang.[150]

Todd returned to the Homestead many times in the final years of Dickinson's life. Lavinia could not help but notice the young woman's praise for her sister's work. Even so, Lavinia first turned to Susan Dickinson for help in getting Emily's poetry published. According to Mabel Loomis Todd, however, Susan was not enthusiastic about the project.

Susan . . . she kept saying she would, & she would perhaps, until Vinnie was wild. At last she announced that she thought nothing had better be done about it, they would never sell—there was not money enough to get them out—the public would not care for them, & so on—in short, she gave it up. Then Vinnie came to me.[151]

Lavinia Dickinson could not have chosen a more ideal person in Amherst, or perhaps anywhere, to work with her sister's poems than Mabel Loomis Todd. For one

Lavinia Dickinson with one of her many cats. After Emily's death, Vinnie decided to find a publisher for her sister's work. Without her determination, Dickinson's work might well have been lost forever.

thing, Todd was a writer of considerable talent. When Lavinia approached her about working on Emily's poetry, Todd had already published a short story. She later went on to publish two volumes of her own poetry, three novels, three travel books, and two science books. Even more important than her professional abilities, perhaps, was Todd's natural affinity for Dickinson's work. Although her life had been very different than Dickinson's, Todd had known her share of heartache, disappointment, and grief. She derived a great deal of comfort from Dickinson's words, she later wrote.

> The poems were having a wonderful effect on me, mentally and spiritually. They seemed to open the door into a wider universe than the little sphere surrounding me which so often hurt and compressed me—and they helped me nobly through a trying time. . . . I was strengthened and uplifted.[152]

As she copied the poems, Todd could not resist changing them to make them read and sound more conventional. When she had finished editing the poems, Todd traveled to Cambridge, Massachusetts, to ask Thomas Wentworth Higginson to help her find a publisher. Higginson at first hesitated. "He did not think a volume advisable," Todd later recalled. "They were too crude in form, he said, and the public would not accept even fine ideas in such rough and mystical dress." Todd disagreed with the famous author's judgment. To prove her point, she read a few of her favorite poems aloud. According to Todd, Higginson was "greatly astonished—he had no idea there were so many in passably conventional form."[153] He agreed to assist with the project.

Together, Todd and Higginson selected 115 poems to make up a first collection. Higginson insisted that they assign titles to the poems, most of which Dickinson had left untitled. The two editors made further changes in Dickinson's work, regularizing her capitalization and punctuation, smoothing her meter, and even changing some of her rhymes.

When he was satisfied that the poems were presentable, Higginson took them to Houghton Mifflin Company, for whom he sometimes read new manuscripts. The editors Higginson approached were not impressed with the work of the unknown poet. They rejected the manuscript, commenting that the poems were "queer—the rhymes were all wrong." [154]

According to David Todd, Mabel Todd's husband, Higginson did not want to take the poems to another publisher in Boston. "Being a reader for Houghton Mifflin, . . . Higginson did not want to ask another Boston publisher to bring out a book which they had turned down," [155] Todd later recalled. Mabel Todd suggested

Mabel Loomis Todd and her husband, David Peck Todd. Inspired by the genius of Dickinson's poetry and moved by its deep emotions, Mabel Loomis Todd worked tirelessly to bring Dickinson's work to the attention of the world. Both of the Todds and even their daughter, Millicent, spent many evenings copying Dickinson's poems to create a publishable manuscript.

that she could send the poems to Thomas Niles, the editor who had seemed so impressed with the poems six years before.

Perhaps Niles had exaggerated his enthusiasm for Dickinson's work in his letters to her. He told Todd that it "had always seemed to him 'most undesirable'" to publish Dickinson's work.[156] However, he agreed to give them to one of the publisher's readers for a second opinion.

"The Real Stuff"

Todd turned to a poet named Arlo Bates. Bates found much to like in Dickinson's manuscript, though he felt the work was greatly flawed. Bates wrote to Todd:

> There is hardly one of these poems which does not bear marks of unusual and remarkable talent; there is hardly one of them which is not marked by an extraordinary crudity of workmanship. There are some poems in the book, however, that are so royally good, and so many that to the poetical will be immensely suggestive, that it seems a pity not to have at least a small edition. . . . Its faults are colossal, but it has the real stuff in no stinted quantities.[157]

Niles reluctantly agreed to bring out a book of Dickinson's poems, provided that the Dickinson family be willing to help pay for the publication. "It has always seemed to me that it would be unwise to perpetuate Miss Dickinson's poems," he wrote to Higginson. "They are quite as remarkable for defects as for beauties & are generally devoid of true poetical qualities. If, however, Miss [Lavinia] Dickinson will pay for the plates, we will publish from them at our ex-

pense a small ed[ition]."[158] Lavinia agreed to the arrangement. Four and a half years after Dickinson's death, Roberts Brothers published *Poems* by Emily Dickinson.

In the decades following the first publication of Dickinson's work, many scholars have criticized Todd and Higginson for daring to edit Dickinson's work. The two have been ridiculed for trying to improve upon works of genius.

These attacks have been somewhat unfair. Once Dickinson became well-known, it was easy to suggest that Higginson and Todd should have left the poems exactly as they found them. When the two collaborators prepared the first manuscript for publication, however, Dickinson was virtually unknown outside of Amherst. They did not know in advance how Dickinson's work would be received. Like a theatrical director who may change the period, costume, and even the setting of a play to give it new life, Higginson and Todd cast Dickinson's poems into a form they thought would capture the imagination of the public. They succeeded.

Many of Higginson and Todd's changes were superficial. For example, they replaced many of Dickinson's dashes with commas, semicolons, colons, and periods. These changes in punctuation alter the appearance of the poem on the page, certainly, but they do not necessarily change how the poem sounds when read aloud. For example, Higginson and Todd removed five of the sixteen dashes in "I taste a liquor never brewed" and replaced the other eleven with conventional punctuation marks. The two versions of the poem look different on the page, but they sound the same when read aloud.

Only when they changed the wording of the poems did Higginson and Todd err gravely. For example, in "This—is the land—the Sunset washes," Dickinson rhymed "Opal Bales" with "Orioles," a fine suspended rhyme.[159] Higginson and Todd replaced "orioles" with "fairy sails" to make a perfect rhyme.[160] Unrealistic and sentimental, this new phrase greatly weakens the poem.

Poetry Torn Up by the Roots

Despite decisions like these, Higginson and Todd were not ignorant of what made Dickinson great. On the contrary, their introductions to Dickinson's books show that they understood Dickinson's gifts perfectly. In his introduction to the 1890 volume, for example, Higginson rightly stresses Dickinson's "unconventional utterance" and "daring thoughts" as distinguishing features of her work. He astutely compared her poetry to that of another great rebel, the English poet William Blake. The beauty of Dickinson's work, he suggests, lies in its raw power.

The first edition of Emily Dickinson's Poems. *The cover design was taken from a painting by Mabel Loomis Todd, which she gave Dickinson in 1882. In return, Dickinson gave Todd a copy of her poem, "A Route of Evanescence."*

> The verses of Emily Dickinson belong emphatically to what Emerson long since called "the Poetry of the Portfolio,"—something produced absolutely without the thought of publication, and solely by way of expression of the writer's own mind. Such verse must inevitably forfeit whatever advantage lies in the discipline of public criticism and the enforced conformity to accepted ways. On the other hand, it may often gain something through the habit of freedom and unconventional utterance of daring thoughts. In the case of the present author, there was absolutely no choice in the matter; she must write thus, or not at all. . . .
>
> It is believed that the thoughtful reader will find in these pages a quality more suggestive of the poetry of William Blake than of anything to be elsewhere found,—flashes of wholly original and profound insight into nature and life; words and phrases exhibiting an extraordinary vividness of descriptive and imaginative power, yet often set in a seemingly whimsical or even

rugged frame. . . . In many cases these verses will seem to the reader like poetry torn up by the roots, with rain and dew and earth still clinging to them, giving a freshness and fragrance not otherwise to be conveyed.[161]

Mabel Loomis Todd's introduction to the second volume of Dickinson's poems, published in 1891, is just as astute as Higginson's introduction to the first. Todd saw that Dickinson's poetry succeeds not in spite of its unconventional form, but because of it.

Like impressionist pictures, or Wagner's rugged music, the very absence of conventional form challenges attention. In Emily Dickinson's exacting hands, the especial, intrinsic fitness of a particular order of words might not be sacrificed to anything virtually extrinsic; and her verses all show a strange cadence of inner rhythmical music. Lines are always daringly constructed, and the "thought-rhyme" appears frequently,—appealing, indeed, to an unrecognized sense more elusive than hearing.[162]

The 1890 book of Dickinson's verse was a popular success. Roberts Brothers reprinted the collection eleven times over the

Mabel Loomis Todd spent countless hours not only editing Dickinson's work, but also promoting it through lectures and articles.

next two years. The publisher immediately contracted for a second volume. Todd and Higginson furnished the publishers with 166 additional poems in 1891. The second book was a success as well. Five years later, Mabel Loomis Todd prepared a third volume of Dickinson's work by herself. It contained another 168 poems. As curiosity about Dickinson as a person grew, Todd prepared a volume of Dickinson's letters for publication. *Letters of Emily Dickinson,* published in 1894, contained 102 more poems and parts of poems, or fragments, along with many of the poet's letters.

The first attempt to present Dickinson's work exactly as she wrote it came in 1914. Martha Dickinson Bianchi, the poet's niece, published *The Single Hound* with few changes in Dickinson's capitalization and punctuation. Bianchi followed this volume with two more—*Further Poems,* published in 1929, and *Unpublished Poems,* in 1935. In 1945 Mabel Loomis Todd's daughter, Millicent Todd Bingham, published *Bolts of Melody,* a collection of 668 of Dickinson's works.

The Poet's Words

In 1950 the Dickinson estate gave the poet's works to Harvard University. Thomas H. Johnson prepared *The Complete Poems of Emily Dickinson* from this literary treasure. Johnson arranged 1,775 of Dickinson's poems and fragments in what he believed to be their chronological order. He found that Dickinson had jotted alternate words or phrases in the margins of many of the poems she had written out. She had also recopied entire poems and inserted changes in them. Johnson included all the variant

readings of the poems in his edition, allowing the reader to enjoy all the different versions of the poems. He describes in detail one of the situations he faced.

> Rare instances exist, notably in the poem "Blazing in gold" (228), where no text can be called "final." That poem describes a sunset which in one version stoops as low as "the kitchen window"; in another, as low as an "oriel window"; in a third, as low as "the Otter's Window." These copies were made over a period of five years from 1861 to 1866, and one text is apparently as "final" as another. The reader may make the choice.[163]

Stephen Crane, the author of The Red Badge of Courage, *was inspired by Dickinson's work to write short, spare poems of his own.*

Johnson recognized the importance of Dickinson's unorthodox punctuation. "Dickinson used dashes as a musical device," he observes, "and though some may be elongated end stops, any 'correction' would be gratuitous." He left the poet's punctuation and capitalization intact. He did, however, correct "obvious misspelling . . . and misplaced apostrophes."[164] The first edition of this groundbreaking work appeared in 1955.

Many poets have been influenced by Dickinson's uncompromising style. After reading the very first edition of Dickinson's poems, Stephen Crane began to write short, spare poems of his own. The author of *The Red Badge of Courage* openly acknowledged his debt to Dickinson. Likewise, Sylvia Plath, a mid-twentieth-century poet, acknowledged her indebtedness to the Amherst poet in a note she attached to a series of poems on the topic of death. Paraphrasing the novelistic disclaimer that reads: "Any similarity to persons real or imagined is purely coincidental," Plath wrote, "Any similarity to Emily Dickinson is purely intentional."[165]

The study of Emily Dickinson has grown in every decade since her death. Dozens of biographies have probed her mind. Hundreds of articles, theses, and critical books have analyzed her technique. One can only imagine the amazement, and possibly amusement, all this attention would have created for the poet who once wrote:

> I'm Nobody! Who are you?
> Are you—Nobody—Too?
> Then there's a pair of us!
> Don't tell! they'd advertise—you know!
>
> How dreary—to be—Somebody!
> How public—like a Frog—
> To tell one's name—the livelong June—
> To an admiring Bog![166]

Notes

Chapter 1: Home

1. Quoted in Thomas H. Johnson and Theodora Ward, eds., *The Letters of Emily Dickinson*, vol. 1. Cambridge, MA: The Belknap Press of Harvard University Press, 1958, pp. 62–63.

2. Quoted in Cynthia Griffin Wolff, *Emily Dickinson*. Reading, MA: Addison-Wesley, 1988, p. 59.

3. Johnson and Ward, eds., *The Letters of Emily Dickinson*, vol. 1, p. 7.

4. Quoted in Jay Leyda, *The Years and Hours of Emily Dickinson*, vol. 1. New Haven, CT: Yale University Press, 1960, pp. 17–18.

5. Johnson and Ward, eds., *The Letters of Emily Dickinson*, vol. 1, p. 13.

6. Quoted in Wolff, *Emily Dickinson*, p. 17.

7. Quoted in Wolff, *Emily Dickinson*, p. 79.

8. Johnson and Ward, eds., *The Letters of Emily Dickinson*, vol. 1, p. 37.

9. Johnson and Ward, eds., *The Letters of Emily Dickinson*, vol. 2, p. 537.

10. Johnson and Ward, eds., *The Letters of Emily Dickinson*, vol. 1, p. 129.

11. Quoted in Leyda, *The Years and Hours of Emily Dickinson*, vol. 2, p. 179.

12. Quoted in Richard B. Sewall, *The Life of Emily Dickinson*. New York: Farrar, Straus and Giroux, 1974, p. 55.

13. Quoted in Wolff, *Emily Dickinson*, p. 31.

14. Johnson and Ward, eds., *The Letters of Emily Dickinson*, vol. 1, p. 231.

15. Millicent Todd Bingham, *Emily Dickinson's Home*. New York: Harper & Brothers, 1955, p. 3.

16. Bingham, *Emily Dickinson's Home*, p. 112.

17. Sewall, *The Life of Emily Dickinson*, p. 62.

18. Johnson and Ward, eds., *The Letters of Emily Dickinson*, vol. 1, p. 148.

19. Johnson and Ward, eds., *The Letters of Emily Dickinson*, vol. 1, p. 111.

20. Johnson and Ward, eds., *The Letters of Emily Dickinson*, vol. 1, p. 144.

21. Johnson and Ward, eds., *The Letters of Emily Dickinson*, vol. 1, p. 161.

22. Thomas H. Johnson, ed., *The Complete Poems of Emily Dickinson*. Boston: Little, Brown & Company, 1957, p. 297.

23. Johnson, ed., *The Complete Poems of Emily Dickinson*, pp. 176–77.

24. Johnson, ed., *The Complete Poems of Emily Dickinson*, p. 553.

25. Johnson and Ward, eds., *The Letters of Emily Dickinson*, vol. 2, pp. 473, 161; vol. 1, pp. 237, 475.

26. Johnson and Ward, eds., *The Letters of Emily Dickinson*, vol. 1, p. 139.

Chapter 2: Heavenly Hurt

27. Johnson and Ward, eds., *The Letters of Emily Dickinson*, vol. 1, p. 53.

28. Quoted in Wolff, *Emily Dickinson*, p. 99.

29. Johnson and Ward, eds., *The Letters of Emily Dickinson*, vol. 1, pp. 59, 62.

30. Johnson and Ward, eds., *The Letters of Emily Dickinson*, vol. 1, p. 54.

31. Quoted in Thomas H. Johnson, *Emily Dickinson, an Interpretive Biography*. Cambridge, MA: The Belknap Press of Harvard University Press, 1963, p. 8.

32. Quoted in Wolff, *Emily Dickinson*, p. 86.

33. Quoted in Leyda, *The Years and Hours of Emily Dickinson*, vol. 1, p. 178.

34. Sewall, *The Life of Emily Dickinson*, p. xxv.

35. Quoted in Wolff, *Emily Dickinson*, p. 100.

36. Johnson and Ward, eds., *The Letters of*

Emily Dickinson, vol. 1, pp. 37–38.

37. Quoted in Leyda, *The Years and Hours of Emily Dickinson*, vol. 1, p. 135.

38. Johnson and Ward, eds., *The Letters of Emily Dickinson*, vol. 1, p. 60.

39. Johnson and Ward, eds., *The Letters of Emily Dickinson*, vol. 1, pp. 67–68.

40. Johnson and Ward, eds., *The Letters of Emily Dickinson*, vol. 1, p. 68.

41. Johnson and Ward, eds., *The Letters of Emily Dickinson*, vol. 1, p. 66.

42. Johnson and Ward, eds., *The Letters of Emily Dickinson*, vol. 1, p. 67.

Chapter 3: A Friend Who Taught Immortality

43. Johnson and Ward, eds., *The Letters of Emily Dickinson*, vol. 1, p. 282.

44. Johnson and Ward, eds., *The Letters of Emily Dickinson*, vol. 2, p. 404.

45. Johnson and Ward, eds., *The Letters of Emily Dickinson*, vol. 1, p. 282.

46. Johnson and Ward, eds., *The Letters of Emily Dickinson*, vol. 2, p. 408.

47. Johnson, ed., *The Complete Poems of Emily Dickinson*, p. 3.

48. Johnson, ed., *The Complete Poems of Emily Dickinson*, p. 3.

49. Johnson, ed., *The Complete Poems of Emily Dickinson*, pp. 5–6.

50. Johnson and Ward, eds., *The Letters of Emily Dickinson*, vol. 1, p. 282.

51. Johnson and Ward, eds., *The Letters of Emily Dickinson*, vol. 2, p. 408.

52. Johnson and Ward, eds., *The Letters of Emily Dickinson*, vol. 2, p. 551.

53. Johnson and Ward, eds., *The Letters of Emily Dickinson*, vol. 1, p. 236.

54. Johnson and Ward, eds., *The Letters of Emily Dickinson*, vol. 1, pp. 282–83.

55. Wolff, *Emily Dickinson*, p. 389.

56. Quoted in Johnson and Ward, eds., *The Letters of Emily Dickinson*, vol. 2, p. 392.

57. Johnson and Ward, eds., *The Letters of Emily Dickinson*, vol. 2, p. 404.

58. Johnson and Ward, eds., *The Letters of Emily Dickinson*, vol. 2, pp. 404, 408.

Chapter 4: Poet

59. Quoted in Richard B. Sewall, *The Lyman Letters: New Light on Emily Dickinson and Her Family*. Amherst, MA: University of Massachusetts Press, 1965, p. 14.

60. Johnson and Ward, eds., *The Letters of Emily Dickinson*, vol. 2, p. 474.

61. Johnson and Ward, eds., *The Letters of Emily Dickinson*, vol. 3, p. 827.

62. Johnson and Ward, eds., *The Letters of Emily Dickinson*, vol. 2, p. 439.

63. Johnson, ed., *The Complete Poems of Emily Dickinson*, pp. ix, viii.

64. Johnson, ed., *The Complete Poems of Emily Dickinson*, p. 27.

65. Johnson and Ward, eds., *The Letters of Emily Dickinson*, vol. 2, p. 412.

66. Johnson and Ward, eds., *The Letters of Emily Dickinson*, vol. 1, p. 32.

67. Johnson and Ward, eds., *The Letters of Emily Dickinson*, vol. 1, p. 282.

68. Johnson, ed., *The Complete Poems of Emily Dickinson*, p. 20.

69. Johnson, ed., *The Complete Poems of Emily Dickinson*, p. viii.

70. Johnson, ed., *The Complete Poems of Emily Dickinson*, p. 44.

71. Johnson, ed., *The Complete Poems of Emily Dickinson*, p. 44.

72. Johnson, ed., *The Complete Poems of Emily Dickinson*, p. 297.

73. Johnson, ed., *The Complete Poems of Emily Dickinson*, pp. 188–89.

74. Johnson, ed., *The Complete Poems of Emily Dickinson*, p. viii.

75. Johnson and Ward, eds., *The Letters of*

Emily Dickinson, vol. 1, p. 144.

76. Johnson, ed., *The Complete Poems of Emily Dickinson*, p. 100.

77. Johnson, ed., *The Complete Poems of Emily Dickinson*, p. 100.

78. Johnson and Ward, eds., *The Letters of Emily Dickinson*, vol. 2, p. 379.

79. Quoted in Johnson and Ward, eds., *The Letters of Emily Dickinson*, vol. 2, pp. 379–80.

80. Quoted in Johnson and Ward, eds., *The Letters of Emily Dickinson*, vol. 2, p. 380.

81. Johnson and Ward, eds., *The Letters of Emily Dickinson*, vol. 2, p. 380.

82. Johnson and Ward, eds., *The Letters of Emily Dickinson*, vol. 2, p. 380.

Chapter 5: Preceptor

83. Quoted in Wolff, *Emily Dickinson*, p. 252.

84. Quoted in Wolff, *Emily Dickinson*, pp. 253–54.

85. Johnson and Ward, eds., *The Letters of Emily Dickinson*, vol. 2, p. 403.

86. Quoted in Johnson, ed., *The Complete Poems of Emily Dickinson*, p. vi.

87. Johnson and Ward, eds., *The Letters of Emily Dickinson*, vol. 2, p. 404.

88. Johnson and Ward, eds., *The Letters of Emily Dickinson*, vol. 2, p. 404.

89. Quoted in Sewall, *The Life of Emily Dickinson*, p. 227.

90. Johnson and Ward, eds., *The Letters of Emily Dickinson*, vol. 2, p. 404.

91. Johnson and Ward, eds., *The Letters of Emily Dickinson*, vol. 2, p. 404.

92. Johnson and Ward, eds., *The Letters of Emily Dickinson*, vol. 2, pp. 404–405.

93. Johnson and Ward, eds., *The Letters of Emily Dickinson*, vol. 2, p. 408.

94. Johnson and Ward, eds., *The Letters of Emily Dickinson*, vol. 2, p. 408.

95. Johnson and Ward, eds., *The Letters of Emily Dickinson*, vol. 2, p. 408.

96. Johnson, ed., *The Complete Poems of Emily Dickinson*, p. 348.

97. Johnson and Ward, eds., *The Letters of Emily Dickinson*, vol. 2, p. 409.

98. Johnson and Ward, eds., *The Letters of Emily Dickinson*, vol. 2, p. 414.

99. Johnson and Ward, eds., *The Letters of Emily Dickinson*, vol. 2, p. 409.

100. Johnson and Ward, eds., *The Letters of Emily Dickinson*, vol. 2, pp. 404, 408.

101. Johnson, ed., *The Complete Poems of Emily Dickinson*, pp. 128, 162, 248, 250, 279, 292.

102. Johnson and Ward, eds., *The Letters of Emily Dickinson*, vol. 2, pp. 409, 460.

Chapter 6: The Soul Selects Her Own Society

103. Johnson and Ward, eds., *The Letters of Emily Dickinson*, vol. 2, p. 419.

104. Johnson and Ward, eds., *The Letters of Emily Dickinson*, vol. 2, p. 460.

105. Quoted in Bingham, *Emily Dickinson's Home*, pp. 413–14.

106. Quoted in Sewall, *The Life of Emily Dickinson*, p. 217.

107. Johnson, ed., *The Complete Poems of Emily Dickinson*, pp. 123, 237, 258, 227.

108. Johnson, ed., *The Complete Poems of Emily Dickinson*, pp. 227–28.

109. Judith Farr, *The Passion of Emily Dickinson*. Cambridge, MA: Harvard University Press, 1992, p. 33.

110. Farr, *The Passion of Emily Dickinson*, pp. 33–34.

111. Quoted in Farr, *The Passion of Emily Dickinson*, p. 40.

112. Wolff, *Emily Dickinson*, p. 507.

113. Johnson, ed., *The Complete Poems of Emily Dickinson*, p. 143.

114. Johnson and Ward, eds., *The Letters of Emily Dickinson*, vol. 2, p. 450.

115. Johnson and Ward, eds., *The Letters of*

Emily Dickinson, vol. 2, p. 450.

116. Johnson and Ward, eds., *The Letters of Emily Dickinson*, vol. 2, p. 453.

117. Quoted in Johnson and Ward, eds., *The Letters of Emily Dickinson*, vol. 2, pp. 461–62.

118. Johnson and Ward, eds., *The Letters of Emily Dickinson*, vol. 2, p. 460.

119. Quoted in Johnson and Ward, eds., *The Letters of Emily Dickinson*, vol. 2, pp. 474, 473.

120. Quoted in Johnson and Ward, eds., *The Letters of Emily Dickinson*, vol. 2, p. 476.

121. Quoted in Johnson and Ward, eds., *The Letters of Emily Dickinson*, vol. 2, p. 476.

122. Quoted in Johnson and Ward, eds., *The Letters of Emily Dickinson*, vol. 2, pp. 473–74.

Chapter 7: Distant Strains of Triumph

123. Johnson and Ward, eds., *The Letters of Emily Dickinson*, vol. 2, p. 526.

124. Quoted in Millicent Todd Bingham, *Ancestors' Brocades*. New York: Harper & Brothers, 1945, p. 233.

125. Quoted in Leyda, *The Years and Hours of Emily Dickinson*, vol. 1, p. 238.

126. Johnson and Ward, eds., The *Letters of Emily Dickinson*, vol. 2, p. 324.

127. Sewall, *The Life of Emily Dickinson*, p. 80.

128. Sewall, *The Life of Emily Dickinson*, p. 81.

129. Johnson and Ward, eds., *The Letters of Emily Dickinson*, vol. 3, p. 675.

130. Johnson and Ward, eds., *The Letters of Emily Dickinson*, vol. 3, pp. 754–55.

131. Johnson and Ward, eds., *The Letters of Emily Dickinson*, vol. 3, p. 746.

132. Quoted in Johnson and Ward, eds., *The Letters of Emily Dickinson*, vol. 2, p. 545.

133. Quoted in Johnson and Ward, eds., *The Letters of Emily Dickinson*, vol. 2, p. 563.

134. Johnson and Ward, eds., *The Letters of Emily Dickinson*, vol. 2, pp. 562–63.

135. Quoted in Johnson and Ward, eds., *The Letters of Emily Dickinson*, vol. 2, p. 564.

136. Johnson and Ward, eds., *The Letters of Emily Dickinson*, vol. 2, p. 566.

137. Quoted in Johnson and Ward, eds., *The Letters of Emily Dickinson*, vol. 2, pp. 624–25.

138. Quoted in Johnson and Ward, eds., *The Letters of Emily Dickinson*, vol. 2, p. 625.

139. Quoted in Johnson and Ward, eds., *The Letters of Emily Dickinson*, vol. 2, p. 626.

140. Quoted in Johnson and Ward, eds., *The Letters of Emily Dickinson*, vol. 3, p. 726.

141. Johnson and Ward, eds., *The Letters of Emily Dickinson*, vol. 3, p. 725.

142. Johnson, ed., *The Complete Poems of Emily Dickinson*, p. 634.

143. Quoted in Johnson and Ward, eds., *The Letters of Emily Dickinson*, vol. 3, p. 769.

144. Johnson, ed., *The Complete Poems of Emily Dickinson*, p. 650.

145. Quoted in Johnson and Ward, eds., *The Letters of Emily Dickinson*, vol. 3, pp. 841–42.

146. Johnson and Ward, eds., *The Letters of Emily Dickinson*, vol. 3, p. 903.

147. Johnson and Ward, eds., *The Letters of Emily Dickinson*, vol. 3, p. 903.

148. Johnson and Ward, eds., *The Letters of Emily Dickinson*, vol. 3, p. 903.

149. Johnson and Ward, eds., *The Letters of Emily Dickinson*, vol. 3, p. 906.

Epilogue: If Fame Belonged to Me

150. Quoted in Sewall, *The Life of Emily Dickinson*, p. 217.

151. Quoted in Sewall, *The Life of Emily Dickinson*, p. 219.

152. Quoted in Sewall, *The Life of Emily Dickinson*, p. 220.

153. Quoted in Sewall, *The Life of Emily Dickinson*, p. 220.

154. Quoted in Bingham, *Ancestors' Brocades*, p. 51.

155. Quoted in Bingham, *Ancestors' Brocades*, p. 51.

156. Quoted in Bingham, *Ancestors' Brocades*, p. 51.

157. Quoted in Bingham, *Ancestors' Brocades*, pp. 52–53.

158. Quoted in Bingham, *Ancestors' Brocades*, p. 53.

159. Johnson, ed., *The Complete Poems of Emily Dickinson*, p. 122.

160. Mabel Loomis Todd and T. W. Higginson, eds., *Favorite Poems of Emily Dickinson*. New York: Avenel Books, 1978, p. 86.

161. Todd and Higginson, eds., *Favorite Poems of Emily Dickinson*, pp. 13, 15–16.

162. Quoted in Sewall, *The Life of Emily Dickinson*, p. 226.

163. Johnson, ed., *The Complete Poems of Emily Dickinson*, p. x.

164. Johnson, ed., *The Complete Poems of Emily Dickinson*, pp. x–xi.

165. Quoted in Helen McNeil, *Emily Dickinson*. New York: Pantheon Books, 1986, p. 130.

166. Johnson, ed., *The Complete Poems of Emily Dickinson*, p. 133.

For Further Reading

Edna Barth, *I'm Nobody! Who Are You?* New York: Ticknor & Fields, A Houghton Mifflin Company, 1971. Barth provides a biography of Emily Dickinson written in a "you were there" style. The book includes eleven complete poems within the text and twenty-three more in a special section in the back.

Emily Dickinson, *I'm Nobody! Who Are You?* Owings Mills, MD: Stemmer House Publishers, 1978. A collection of especially accessible poems written by Emily Dickinson and illustrated by Rex Schneider. The book includes an excellent introduction by noted Dickinson scholar Richard B. Sewall.

Aileen Fisher and Olive Rabe, *We Dickinsons.* New York: Atheneum, 1965. The book presents the life of Emily Dickinson "as seen through the eyes of her brother Austin." Rich in detail, the book was not actually written by the supposed narrator, of course. As a result, the narrative often raises questions rather than answering them.

Tamara Johnson, *Readings on Emily Dickinson.* San Diego: Greenhaven, 1997. An anthology of essays that provides literary analysis and criticism of the poems of Emily Dickinson.

Works Consulted

Millicent Todd Bingham, *Ancestors' Brocades.* New York: Harper & Brothers, 1945. A detailed account by the daughter of Mabel Loomis Todd of how the first volumes of Dickinson's poetry came to be published. Bingham draws heavily on her mother's diary, journal, and correspondence, as well as on interviews with her father and others to illuminate every aspect of the poet's "literary debut."

Millicent Todd Bingham, *Emily Dickinson's Home.* New York: Harper & Brothers, 1955. Using the contents of a camphor wood chest stuffed with the Dickinson family's letters that she inherited from her mother, Bingham provides a detailed look at life in the Dickinson household.

Judith Farr, *The Passion of Emily Dickinson.* Cambridge, MA: Harvard University Press, 1992. "Not a biography," in the words of the author, this book provides a fascinating study of Dickinson's life, work, and aesthetic, emphasizing Dickinson's interest in the visual arts. The chapters devoted to "The Narrative of Sue" and "The Narrative of Master" are especially interesting.

Albert J. Gelpi, *Emily Dickinson, The Mind of the Poet.* New York: W. W. Norton, 1971. Gelpi presents a dense, well-argued discussion of the poet as a strong-willed, atheistic pessimist.

Thomas H. Johnson, ed., *The Collected Letters of Emily Dickinson.* Cambridge, MA: The Belknap Press of Harvard University Press, 1958. A representative sample of the letters first published in *The Letters of Emily Dickinson.*

Thomas H. Johnson, ed., *The Complete Poems of Emily Dickinson.* Boston: Little, Brown & Company, 1957. In this reader's version of the 1955 variorum text, Johnson offers "but one form of each poem."

Thomas H. Johnson, *Emily Dickinson, an Interpretive Biography.* Cambridge, MA: The Belknap Press of Harvard University Press, 1963. A concise presentation of the poet's life by the editor who brought the world the first complete, unaltered edition of Dickinson's poetry.

Thomas H. Johnson, ed., *The Poems of Emily Dickinson.* Cambridge, MA: The Belknap Press of Harvard University Press, 1955. An unreconstructed presentation of all 1,775 of Dickinson's poems, fragments, and variants.

Thomas H. Johnson and Theodora Ward, eds., *The Letters of Emily Dickinson.* Vols. 1–3. Cambridge, MA: The Belknap Press of Harvard University Press, 1958. An annotated collection of the 1,045 letters known at the time to have been written by the poet.

Jay Leyda, *The Years and Hours of Emily Dickinson.* Vols. 1–2. New Haven, CT: Yale University Press, 1960. As the title suggests, the author provides a year-by-year and sometimes hour-by-hour chronology of the poet's life.

Helen McNeil, *Emily Dickinson.* New York: Pantheon Books, 1986. The author mingles "feminism, literary analysis, poststructuralism, and what one might call the new rhetorical criticism" to provide a fresh view of Dickinson as a shrewd, strong, innovative artist. Includes interesting photographs, including two of Dickinson's manuscript pages.

Richard B. Sewall, *The Life of Emily Dickinson.* New York: Farrar, Straus and Giroux, 1974. Originally published in two volumes, Sewall's book remains the definitive biography of the poet.

Richard B. Sewall, *The Lyman Letters: New Light on Emily Dickinson and Her Family.* Amherst, MA: University of Massachusetts Press, 1965. The famous Dickinson biographer uses the letters of Joseph Lyman to explore the workings of the Dickinson household.

Mabel Loomis Todd and T. W. Higginson, eds., *Favorite Poems of Emily Dickinson.* New York: Avenel Books, 1978. A facsimile reproduction of Dickinson's first book of poems, including Higginson's introduction. The book also contains a few selections from Dickinson's *Poems, Second Series.*

Cynthia Griffin Wolff, *Emily Dickinson.* Reading, MA: Addison-Wesley, 1988. Wolff's in-depth biography provides a wealth of information about Dickinson's life and times. The book is burdened with speculation, however, especially Wolff's thesis that the infant Dickinson was deprived of "eye/face dialogue" with her mother and that it was "this disruption of this earliest form of unvoiced communication that lingered in her creative imagination."

James Playsted Wood, *Emily Elizabeth Dickinson, a Portrait.* Nashville, TN: T. Nelson, 1972. A well-written and deceptively simple account of the poet's life.

Index

After Great Pain (Cody), 68–69

agoraphobia, 61

Alcott, Louisa May, 72

Amherst Academy, 13, 15–16, 24

Amherst College, 16, 19, 34, 76

Amherst Record, 18

Atlantic Monthly, 21, 52–53, 66–67

Bates, Arlo, 79

Bianchi, Martha Dickinson, 62, 82

Bingham, Millicent Todd, 20, 78, 82

Blake, William, 80

Bolts of Melody (Todd/Bingham), 82

Bowdoin, Elbridge, 35

Bowles, Samuel, 56, 60, 74
  publishes Emily's poems, 51, 65

Brontë sisters, 22, 33, 35, 73

Browning, Elizabeth Barrett, 22, 52

Browning, Robert, 22

Bullard, O. A., 12, 18

Child, Lydia Marie, 33

Cody, John, 68–69

Coleman, Eliza, 39

Complete Poems of Emily Dickinson (Johnson), 42, 72, 82

Congregationalists, 26, 28–29, 32, 36

Crane, Stephen, 83

Daily Republican. See Springfield *Daily Republican*

Dickens, Charles, 22

Dickinson, Austin (William), 11–12, 22, 47–48, 55, 57
  education of, 14, 15, 20, 21
  Emily's letters to, 13–14, 20–23, 27, 30, 36–38
  relationship to father, 19–20, 21, 68

Dickinson, Edward, 11, 22–23
  as attorney, 16, 32
  as community leader, 18–19
  as Congregationalist, 26, 28
  as elected official, 16, 18, 39, 52
  as father, 16, 18, 19–21, 48, 68

Dickinson, Emily Elizabeth
  as poet, 42–43, 45, 47, 48–51, 59
    publishing and, 57–58, 70–74
    seclusion of, 60–61, 64, 66, 76
    seeks guidance, 53, 54
    white clothing of, 61–64, 76
    writing techniques of, 12, 35, 45–47, 58, 83
    capitalization as, 46–47
  childhood of, 11, 13, 14
  death of, 75
  education of, 15–16, 24–26, 31
  home of, 11–12, 21, 41–42
  photos of, 11, 61, 65
  letters of
    adult, 32, 36–37, 40–42, 44
      Valentine letter, 34
    childhood, 13–15
    during seclusion, 60
    teenage, 13, 16–18, 21
      about parents, 20–23, 38
      about Sophia Holland, 19, 44
      at Mount Holyoke, 24–31
    to Thomas Higginson, 53–60, 65–66, 69, 71
    see also Letters of Emily Dickinson
  poems of, 12, 18, 40
    influence of, 12, 83
    interpretations of, 43–46, 47, 48, 50
    numbers of, 12, 42, 45, 47, 48, 53, 55, 59, 65, 76
    publishing of, 57–58, 70–74, 76–83
      by Roberts Brothers, 72, 79, 81–82

by Springfield *Daily Republican*, 35, 51, 65
  changes made during, 77–80
  themes in, 35, 45, 69
  see also poetry
portraits of, 12, 16, 29, 33, 42
relationships, with
  Dickinson, Sue, 47–51
  father, 20, 22–23, 69, 70
  Higginson, Thomas, 53–60, 65–67, 71, 75
  Jackson, Helen Hunt, 70–72, 75
  mother, 68–70
  Newton, Ben, 32–33, 35–36, 38–40, 43, 56
  Niles, Thomas, 72–74
  Wadsworth, Charles, 39–40, 51, 61–63
spiritual journey of
  at home, 16, 18
  at Mount Holyoke, 24–25, 28–31
  in later years, 33, 36, 38–40, 56
  teenage years of, 13, 21–22, 55
  at Mount Holyoke Seminary, 24–31
Dickinson, Emily Norcross, 11, 21, 28, 41, 74
  health of, 68–69
Dickinson, Lavinia Norcross (Vinnie)
  childhood of, 11, 12, 15, 22, 33
  later years of, 39, 41, 61
    as caregiver, 69
    seeks publisher, 76–77, 79

on Emily as poet, 42, 61
Dickinson, Samuel Fowler, 13–15, 16, 61
Dickinson, Susan Gilbert, 47–51, 58, 65
  as Emily's critic, 48–49, 76–77
  Emily's letters to, 21, 74
  on Emily's seclusion and, 61, 63
Dickinson, Thomas Gilbert, 74
Dickinson, Willie, 74

Eliot, George, 73
Emerson, Ralph Waldo, 21–22, 33, 72, 73, 75
Emily Dickinson's Home (Bingham), 20
Evans, Marian, 73

Farr, Judith, 50, 62–63
Further Poems (Bianchi), 82

Gilbert, Sandra M., 63
Golden Legend (Longfellow), 48
Gould, George, 28
Gubar, Susan, 63

Hale, Edward Everett, 38–39
Harvard Law School, 20, 21
Haven, Mary Emerson, 45
Higginson, Thomas Wentworth, 52–59, 71, 77–78
  as author, 52–53
  as editor, 78, 79–80, 82
  as Emily's critic, 53–54, 57, 58
  as Emily's friend, 59, 75

on Emily, 64, 66–67
  on Emily's poetry, 80–81
Hitchcock, Edward, 16
Holland, Josiah Gilbert, 56
Holland, Mrs. J. G., 70
Holland, Sophia, 19, 43–44
Houghton Mifflin Company, 78
Howland, William, 35, 36
Humphrey, Jane, 13
Humphrey, Leonard, 43–44

Indicator, 34

Jackson, Helen Hunt, 70–72, 75
Jackson, William S., 75
Jane Eyre (Brontë), 35
Johnson, Thomas H., 14, 43–44, 82–83
  on number of poems, 42, 45, 47, 59

Kavanaugh (Longfellow), 22
Keats, John, 22
King, Stanley, 19

Letters of Emily Dickinson (Johnson/Ward)
  Thomas Higginson in, 64
  to Abiah Root, 17, 19, 25, 40
  to her brother, 14, 27, 30, 37, 38
  to Louise Norcross, 44
  to Thomas Higginson, 54, 59, 69
  Valentine letter in, 34

Letters of Emily Dickinson
    (Todd), 82
Life and Letters of Emily
    Dickinson, 62
Life of Emily Dickinson
    (Sewall), 69
Lind, Jenny, 37
Literary World, 72
Longfellow, Henry
    Wadsworth, 21, 22, 48
Lord, Otis P., 74–75
Lyman, Joseph, 41
Lyon, Mary, 24–26, 29, 30
    religious survey of, 28

Madwoman in the Attic
    (Gilbert/Gubar), 63
Masque of Poets (Niles), 72
Moser, Barry, 42
Mount Holyoke Female
    Seminary, 24–26

Newton, Ben, 32–33,
    35–36, 51
Niles, Thomas, 72–74, 78–79
Norcross, Betsy, 11
Norcross, Emily, 29
Norcross, Frances, 68, 75
Norcross, Joel, 11
Norcross, Lavinia, 13, 26,
    28
Norcross, Louise, 44, 68, 75

Passion of Emily Dickinson
    (Farr), 62
Philosophy of Housekeeping
    (Lyman), 41
Plath, Sylvia, 83
Poems (Dickinson), 79, 80
Poems (Emerson), 33
Poems, First Series, 47
Poems of Emily Dickinson
    (Johnson), 47, 50, 56

poetry, 43, 67
    "A darting fear—a
        pomp—a tear—," 45
    "Adrift! A little boat
        adrift!," 44
    "A precious—mouldering
        pleasure—'tis," 22
    "How happy is the little
        Stone," 73
    "Hurrah for Peter
        Parley!," 36
    "I'll tell you how the Sun
        rose—," 56
    "I'm Nobody! Who are
        you?," 83
    "I never lost as much but
        twice," 43
    "Me to adorn—How—
        tell," 62
    "One Sister have I in our
        house," 50
    "Pass to thy Rendezvous
        of Light," 74
    "Safe in their Alabaster
        Chambers," 48–50
    "Some keep the Sabbath
        going to Church—," 47
    "South Winds jostle
        them—," 45
    "Success is counted
        sweetest," 72
    "The Soul selects her
        own Society," 65
    "The Spider holds a
        Silver Ball," 46

Red Badge of Courage, The
    (Crane), 83
Roberts Brothers, 70–72,
    79, 81–82
Root, Abiah, 28, 31
    Emily's letters to, 15–19,
        24–26, 28–30, 31, 40, 44

Round Table, 47
Ruskin, John, 22

Scribner's Monthly, 56
Sewall, Richard, B., 20,
    69–70
Shakespeare, William, 22,
    64
Shipley, Henry, 34
Single Hound (Bianchi), 82
Springfield *Daily*
    Republican, 21, 56
    Emily's poems in, 35, 51,
        65
Stoddard, Solomon, 26
Stowe, Harriet Beecher,
    22

Todd, David Peck, 76, 78
Todd, Mabel Loomis,
    76–82
    as editor, 77–78, 79–80,
        82
    on Emily, 55, 76
    on Emily's poetry, 76, 77,
        81
Tolman, Susan L., 28
Tuckerman, Frederick, 15

Unitarian Church, 32–33,
    36
Unpublished Poems
    (Bianchi), 82

Wadsworth, Reverend
    Charles, 39–40, 51, 74
Ward, Theodora, 14
Whitman, Walt, 55
Whittier, John Greenleaf,
    72
Wolff, Cynthia Griffin, 39,
    63
Wood, Abby, 29, 40

Credits

Pictures

Cover photo: Robert Frost Library

Amherst College Archives and Special Collections, 27, 33

Amherst History Museum, 63 (bottom)

Beinecke Library, Yale University, 80

Corbis-Bettmann, 37

The Emily Dickinson Homestead, 65

By permission of the Houghton Library, Harvard University, 12, 18, 21, 43, 46, 48, 49, 53, 55, 60, 61

J. Sommer Coll./Archive Photos, 29

Library of Congress, 16, 70, 82

Special Collections, The Jones Library, Inc., Amherst, MA, 11, 15, 26, 39, 41, 42, 52, 63 (top), 68, 69, 77

Stock Montage, Inc., 24

Todd Bingham Collection, Yale University Library, 31, 58, 74, 78, 81

Text

About the Author

Bradley Steffens is a widely published poet and the author of fourteen books for young readers. He attended Macalester College, where he took an independent study course in Emily Dickinson taught by the late Roger K. Blakely. As part of the course, Steffens composed several poems in the manner of Emily Dickinson, a few of which have seen their way into print. Steffens lives in Poway, California, with his wife, Angela, and children, Ezekiel, Tessa, and John.